Managing Professionals?
Don't!

Managing Professionals? Don't!

HOW TO STEP BACK TO GO FORWARD

A CONTINENTAL EUROPEAN PERSPECTIVE

Mathieu Weggeman

and

Cees Hoedemakers

Warden Press

© 2014 Mathieu Weggeman and Cees Hoedemakers
ISBN:
Paperback: 978-94-92004-01-7
E-book (Epub): 978-94-92004-07-9
E-book (Mobi/Kindle): 978-94-92004-08-6
Original title: *Leidinggeven aan professionals? Niet doen! Over kenniswerkers, vakmanschap en innovatie.* Schiedam: Scriptum 2007
This edition published by Warden Press / Wardy Poelstra, Amsterdam
Translated from the Dutch by Cees Hoedemakers and Jonathan Ellis
Cover design: Sander Pinkse, Amsterdam
Cover photo: courtesy Harry Bloemink, Patty Boomstra, Nicolette Lucassen, and our unknown friend at De Baak, Training and Knowledge Institute in the field of leadership and entrepreneurship, Driebergen.
Interior design / lay-out: Elgraphic bv, Vlaardingen

TABLE OF CONTENTS

Introduction   3

1 MISSION AND VISION   11
Improve the balance: More collective ambition,
fewer rules and procedures

2 STRATEGY   46
The strategy is: Innovation and operational excellence
and customer focus

3 STRUCTURE   61
Stimulate borderless collaboration through loosely
defined and multiform structures

4 SYSTEMS   90
Do not manage based on process but on desired output:
Do so with the aid of Personal and Team Commitment
Statements

5 PEOPLE   108
Offer professionals continuing learning opportunities
to ensure state-of-the-art involvement in their profession

6 MANAGEMENT STYLE   139
Inspire professionals, BE there, dare to differentiate,
function as heat shield against "noise from above"'
and love their profession

7 ORGANIZATIONAL CULTURE 170
*Stimulate a climate in which professionals are trusted
and given room to exploit and explore their profession*

Grand Finale 185

Bibliography 187

Introduction

This book is about the art and the science of managing professionals and why it is not all that necessary. However, the few things that are necessary should be done well. Managers must be there only at the right moment, not before and not after. That requires great alertness, good timing and a healthy dose of modesty. If there are many opportunities to score, the chance of getting applause is larger than if there are only a few windows of opportunity to score. This book wants to help managers of professionals with this. We do that with a bit of theory and lots of real-life examples and anecdotes in seven chapters that coincide with the aspects that determine the organization and administration of an organization or department and that represent the managers' working areas: mission and vision (1), strategy (2), structure (3), systems, rules and procedures (4), employees and their knowledge (5), management style (6) and organizational culture (7).

Managers should take care not to make things worse

"You can't improve research quality by organizing better.
Suppose a group of people is capable of performing at a level arbitrarily set at 100. There is nothing you can do organizationally that will make them perform at 110, but there certainly are things that you can do that will make them perform at 90 or 80 or even at 10."
Martin Thomas, Vice President of the Australian Academy of Technological Sciences and Engineering

Who will benefit from this book?
Generally larger organizations or parts thereof and networks with predominantly professionals, like broadcasting, multimedia, newspaper and magazine publishers, hospitals, and other organizations in the

health care sector, R&D departments and laboratories, high tech enterprises, electronics and automotive companies, research institutes, universities, and other educational and training centers, architects, automation and organization consultancies and design firms, IT and telecommunications companies, accounting firms, law firms and tax consultancies, orchestras, theater groups, the film, entertainment and other creative industries, cultural organizations, ministries, state administrations and city councils, police, fire departments, and other security organizations, lobby groups and many more.

This book is not relevant for:
- small organizations like high tech start-ups and start-ups in the creative industry;
- sports organizations where it is all about power and hierarchy;
- organizations where the production factor of physical labor is dominant, such as in hotels, bars and restaurants, fishery, agriculture, and construction, as well as slaughter houses, carpentries and cleaning firms;
- routinely working organizations like licensing firms, supermarkets and other shops, highway rest areas, front offices, banks, call centers, security firms, etc.

Working in the Rhineland tradition
In this book, we will talk a lot about the so-called *Rhineland Way*. The Rhineland Way was French philosopher Michel Albert's proposed answer to the Anglo-American style of market capitalism that spread across the globe after the demise of Communism in the early 1990s. "The Rhineland work culture is directed at the professional content of the activities and the achievement of a social consensus between employers, employees, and financers" (Albert, 1991).

Today, in the wake of recent scandals and the crisis in the banking industry, this alternative is more viable – and more needed – than ever before. The Rhineland Way is a Continental European style of leadership and organization. It is based on principles instead of rules, proclaims to trust the skilled craftsman and to focus on primary processes.

For Rhineland leaders, long-term continuity is more important than short-term profits, and their love of the profession of the workers and the products they make is greater than their love of money and power.

An organization should not be just a money-making machine, but a place where skilled workers enjoy the beauty of craftsmanship to satisfy their customers.

The Rhineland work culture

In the Rhineland tradition, managerial authority is awarded based on ability and is more a bottom-up than a top-down process. The origins of this process can be found in the guild system that functioned in the late Middle Ages. The guilds at that time made a distinction between three levels of ability: pupil, companion/apprentice (trainee), and master. The latter had shown that he was an accomplished craftsman by making his masterpiece. The test of ability was held in front of all the qualified masters; it was an early example of what we now call peer review. The title of Master earned someone the right to distribute the large amount of work required for complicated products among the trainees and to assess the quality of the work they produced. Even to-day, the line manager in Rhineland organizations is a professional who spends part of his time working in a primary process and who has been asked to undertake certain management tasks because he, compared to his colleagues, has an above-average level of social and communication skills. The Anglo-American first-line supervisor is more a "hands-off" knowledge broker than a knowledge worker and is selected because of his MBA-like abilities, one of the most important of which is deciding on quantitative measures (spreadsheet management).

Companies in the New World concentrate on satisfying shareholders and therefore on short-term profits. This short-term orientation goes at the expense of R&D and investments to reach state-of-the art competences of personnel. Organizations that work according to the Rhineland model concentrate on satisfied customers *and* satisfied employees *and* satisfied shareholders and are thus more concerned with long-term continuity. Partly because of this, the social differences are smaller and there is, on the whole, relatively more attention given to schooling and practical training (see, for example, the German apprenticeship model that is open to everybody and is funded by corporate life).

The Anglo-American Business Model	The Rhineland Work Culture
Minimum government intervention	Social consensus between employers, employees and financiers
Directed at short-term profit (shareholder value)	Directed at long-term continuity (satisfied customers, employees and shareholders)
Role model is the entrepreneurial, successful, heroic CEO	Belief in the strength of the collective
The organization is a money-making machine	Organization is a necessary evil for the realization of complex products
Power and command & control are important	Craftsmanship is important
Professional ability is the responsibility of the employee	Professional ability is the responsibility of the employee and the company
Focus on engineering and manufacturing processes; more technology-driven	Focus on innovation; more science-driven
The manager is an MBA because managing is a trade; the one who is the boss decides	The manager is an actively involved foreman; managing is not a trade; the one who knows decides
Management appointments are top-down; support is bottom-up	Management appointments are middle-up-down; support is derived from the primary process
Managerial language is made up of abstract and catchy jargon	Management language deals with products and the actual processes on the floor
Public image: adventurous, exciting, passionate and attractive to the media	Public image: careful, thoughtful, virtuous and dull
Danger: bureaucratic rigidity through a vast number of rules, procedures and lawyers	Danger: anarchy and the organization as a playground due to an excess of artistry

Finally and for clarity, the following lists choices and assumptions that were made in writing this book:

- Professionals include so-called *knowledge workers*: those professionals that have an academic degree for whom the production factor knowledge in their brain is more important than their ability to do physical labor. Having said that, for the sake of variation we use the terms "knowledge workers" and "professionals" as synonyms, except when the context requires a specific distinction.
- Strategy refers to standard strategy in its broadest sense, covering mission (why) + vision (where to) + objective (what) + strategy in a strict sense (how). In case of an action plan to achieve predetermined goals, we use the word strategy in its strict sense.
- And finally: we have not made the distinction between he and she. Where it says he you can read she and vice versa.

How to manage professionals

This book is about the art and knowledge of managing professionals and why that is not strictly necessary. However, the few things that are necessary must be done well. Managers are only required to be there at the precise moment, not earlier and not later. That demands great alertness, good timing and considerable discretion. If you have many scoring chances, the chance of applause is greater than when you have only a few windows of opportunity. This book helps managers solve this difficult task by using a touch of theory combined with numerous real-life examples, cases and anecdotes in seven parts. These parts correspond to the seven characteristics that determine the structure and control of an organization or department and hence represent managers' work areas: mission and vision (1), strategy (2), structure (3), systems, rules and procedures (4), employees and their knowledge (5), its own management style (6) and organizational culture (7).

The main recommendations are given in the imperative voice since exaggeration tends to help when making clarifications.

1 MISSION AND VISION

Improve the balance: More collective ambition, fewer rules and procedures

The message for knowledge-intensive organizations:

The bad news:
Professionals are impossible to manage by imposing rules and procedures or by information systems (Mintzberg, 1979)

The good news:
The energy level of professionals is a function of their potential to identify with the "values" or higher goals of the organization

The result of both is known as mission or **collective ambition.**

First the "bad news." "Old hat," you might say, based on research from way back in 1979, when Henry Mintzberg first formulated this so clearly that subsequently everyone suddenly saw how true this was – so honor to whom honor is due. Numerous studies have since led to variations on the same conclusion for a variety of occupational groups (policy officers, lawyers, engineers) and for a variety of types of organizations (hospitals, R&D laboratories, ministries). And it is bad news because the top three instruments which management uses to keep personnel in check are still: **rules, procedures and information systems**. Maybe you think: "It's time to stop all this nonsense. I will prove Mintzberg's theory wrong at my company, thank you very much!" Well, good luck to you. But don't expect a good time.

Professionals, however, do not really think it is such "bad news." That is why "bad news" is put in quotation marks. Mintzberg is, among laymen, the best-known organization scientist, for the very reason of the research cited here. If the manager of a law practice says enthusiastically: "We have designed a new digital form to register certain variables online," there is a very good chance that the professionals will say: "Haven't you read Mintzberg? It won't work here!" That's how they misuse our old friend!

Despite setting up self-regulating teams, result-accountable units, internal entrepreneurship, empowerment and the like, organizations are still overloaded with rules and procedures. The question is what for? Whatever it is, it is not good for the innovation of products, services and processes and it frustrates entrepreneurship. Rules and procedures limit the freedom of action, force unknown problems into the straight jacket of existing solutions and oppose exceptions and changes.

Is a more anarchy-tainted management style an alternative? Probably not. Obviously, the challenge is to create a balance between anarchy and planning & control.

The professionals' irritation is not so much caused by "horizontal rules." These include security procedures and trade-disciplinary standards, directives, step-by-step plans and protocols. The stuff engineers, educators and doctors use internally when exercising their profession. The real trouble is caused by "vertical rules." Rules and procedures used by management in trying to plan and control professional work processes. The "vertical rules" support the strategic autonomy (*what* to do) and the resultant accountability of management. The "horizontal rules" influence the professional autonomy (*how* to do it) and the nature and the scope of the effort and commitment of the professional. Given this, and depending on the expertise and attitude of the professional, it is possible that such interference can be experienced either as supportive or as obstructive.

"The reason your workers follow you is not because you're providing some mysterious leadership. It's because you're following them ..."

Lee Iacocca talking about his work at Chrysler.

Horizontal and vertical control

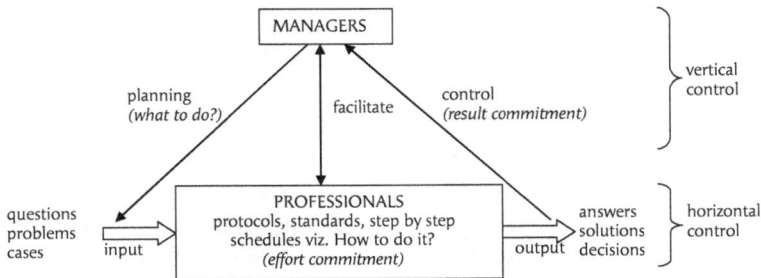

These two systems of control can easily come into conflict with each other. This happens most of all where they come into closest contact with each other: in the workplace. It is not so much the tension between strategic (*what*) and professional (*how*) autonomy which causes problems; it is the relative incompatibility of management's commitment to results and professionals' commitment to effort.

Obliging professionals to produce results in the hope of avoiding conflicts between vertical and horizontal control is no solution. That is simply self-deception because it is impossible to see from the results of work whether a professional has done his job properly. A judge cannot guarantee that a convict who has served out his sentence will not offend again; a management consultant cannot promise a company that it will make more profit after setting up a shared service center, and a cured patient can get sick again next week.

It is my impression that, as a result of the increasing appetite for control – for the dominant paradigm of management is still: planning & control – professionals protest less and less against all those rules and procedures and simply go along with them. They have discovered that "being against things" costs more energy than simply cheating the system. That behavior was once referred to in a large engineering department where I worked as "collaborative opposition."

Subversion starts innocently enough with the application of the DELLE principle, invented by the over-organized Germans. It is an acronym for *Durch Einfach Liegen Lassen, Erledigen* which means "to solve something by just leaving it alone." And indeed, most of the forms received in the mail can be deleted, without anyone ever noticing their absence.

BOHICA is an acronym of a similar type. It is most frequently used when a newly appointed manager dreams up an idea for enforcing greater control – an idea also dreamed up by his three predecessors and which, each of those three times, proved a total failure. Professionals advise each other to adopt the BOHICA attitude: Bend Over, Here It Comes Again.

Stimulated by the time gains achieved through such relatively innocent practices, people set in motion more severe forms of "cheating." I will mention a few real-life examples; the names have been changed to protect the ...

Much ado at Casey Labs

"I agree with your observation that it is difficult, if not impossible, to manage professionals by imposing rules and procedures," nodded sector director C. Marino of Casey Labs in agreement.

"Even worse," he continued, "they are no longer even against things, because being against things costs more time than simply playing along with the game. To give an example: each year the group leaders – and this applies to all sectors within the lab – must present a group plan in which they indicate, with clear arguments, what they are planning to do in the coming year. Such a group plan must satisfy a number of clearly defined conditions and forms the basis for the allocation of the group's budget. Mind you, you shouldn't read too much into this because more than 70% of that budget consists of personnel costs and obviously the people are there already, so there's not a lot still to be decided based on the group plan. Most group leaders find drawing up the plan a rather useless and annoying task. What's more, it has to be accurate because it contains a number of interrelated functions such as projects versus capacities and so on, and these must be correct. Recently I found out, purely by accident, that one of my group leaders had delegated this task to a junior colleague who had just joined the company and had some spare time on his hands. He had given him the group plan for the current year plus a copy of the traditional autumn address by the general director for research. He always listed 10 key focus points for the coming period and the junior colleague was told to more or less copy the current plan and, if the opportunity presented itself, incorporate some of those key points. Not all ten, of course – that would attract suspicion – but say six or seven. He could send the "new" plan directly "upstairs" – the group leader did not need to see it – because there was "staff" up there who would do all sorts of things with the plan, the group leader had told his bright-eyed junior: calculating, comparing with other group plans, tray-in-tray-out, put the data in Excel and make pie-charts from it. In any case they wouldn't hear anything for the coming six months, and that didn't matter because they all knew what they were doing. So you see, Mr. Weggeman, that's the way things happen here."

Marino looked out of the window, his hands in his pockets, gazed up at the ceiling, then to the points of his Italian shoes and said, while balancing on his heels: "In a way, I can understand the guys. Some years back we had just one single department number for all the different research sectors: 860.41, and in the Scientific Executive Board meeting there was only one real criterion: there is always money for a good project. Now that we have started with separate budgets for each group, I sometimes wonder whether that criterion still applies."

"Naturally, when I found out about this, I confronted the group leader in question. I told him: 'If you don't think those group plans are worth very much, you should tell me to my face – and then we can discuss it together.' His answer was: 'Well, I knew that you would say that I had a point because my group didn't really need it at all but that there are a lot of other groups around that really need to make such a plan and that you cannot make exceptions because that sets a precedent – by the way, I've never really understood that; I'll just keep on setting precedents, so in the end there won't be any more precedents – and in the end I'll still have to do it. So let's save each other the bother of that discussion. You'll get your group plan, but please don't expect me to put my best people on it. We all know exactly what is expected of us. We don't need a group plan to tell us that. But you've got a complete collection of support staff upstairs and they need data to process, otherwise they have nothing to do. So you'll get my data, but it serves no purpose whatsoever in the group.' And then he subtly mentioned Parkinson's Law: $W_s = f(T_w)$: support staff work is a linear function of the time which is available for that work. So you see, professor, managing is not a walk in the park.'"

Parkinson's Law is still extremely topical

Staff is: management support, HR, IT, finances, administration, legal, communication, services, etc.

A 2006 Berenschot management consultancy study into the effects of a large versus a small workforce showed that:
- Public organizations (such as local authorities, care foundations, or schools) with relatively a large support staff do not deliver a better quality product than organizations with small overheads; they are just more expensive.

- Difficulties can arise with both an extremely large and an extremely small workforce.
- In situations where the workforce is extremely small, the mood of the day prevails and fire fighting is rife.
- In situations where the workforce is extremely large, we see "lots of bureaucracy, an excess of control, interference, an excess of new policy and a constant start-up of new developments."

... but no request was made!

The supervisor of a group of biologists once told me about a recent experience he had had with the bureaucracy at his institute. "You see," he said, "we sit here in an old but attractive building with windows that you can open by sliding them up and down. Due to wear and tear, the frames are not always parallel which means that, depending on the temperature, we cannot always open or close the windows. The incident occurred last February during a rain storm. For some reason, the windows of the computer room on the third floor had been opened that morning and we could not close them. As a result the wind blew the rain in and much of our expensive equipment got wet. In the old days, you simply called maintenance and they would come and close the windows. Not anymore; we've had consultants here and we now have Facilities Management, and that works completely differently. I immediately called their "front desk" – another invention – and told them about our problem and asked if they could come and fix it. "We can't do that," they said, "because no request form has been issued." "Yes," I said, thinking I had a valid point, "but the rain's falling on the computers." "Then you'd better put some plastic over it, because no request form has been filed and unless you file one, our hands are tied. We can't react to each telephone call just like that. That would be crazy. That is why we introduced these new procedures with form pads."

We started hunting around for the form pad and finally found one in a bottom drawer somewhere and quickly filled one out and then they came. The next day I arranged for a meeting with all department heads and told them the story. "This will never happen again," we decided. We ordered a few more pads and filled them all out with every conceivable thing that could go wrong including tsunamis and meteor hits. We took them to the Facilities Management with a grin on our faces. "Now things are just like they were before," we explained to them. "Whenever something happens we phone you and say: 'Can you come, the form has been filled out and all you have to do is fill in the date.' After that we had no more problems. When in need you simply help one another, don't you?"

Long live the random generator

After submitting and resubmitting, clarifying, defending and again submitting numerous letters, a research consortium finally succeeded in securing an externally financed European Union project that provided work for three years. They were prepared to jump through all the necessary bureaucratic hoops because they were intrinsically motivated by the complexity of the project. But the celebrations soon gave way to the hangover; all project teams concerned had to log their time in units of 6 minutes. Here again Parkinson's Law applies. The subsidizing organization had so many administrative staff, accountants, auditors (actually accountants checking the other accountants) that they needed an enormous amount of data to keep them busy. "Time logging in units of 6 minutes for a project that lasts three years? That implies a huge loss of time! [They had, of course, forgotten to include the time for filling in the forms in the project application.] So of course we're not going to do that," said the researchers. And so they first invested in writing a computer program that would produce fake but credible timesheets. At the start of the project each project member had to provide some personal information (sub-projects he/she was working on, his/her allocation factors in the project, the most likely holiday periods and days off, whether you were an early starter and an early leaver, or the other way around, someone who took long lunches, etc) and then the random generator took care of the rest. One day you went to lunch at half past twelve, the next at five to twelve. One day you left at a quarter past four and the next day you worked until seven. The program processed things in such a way that at the end of the month the accumulated time logging data was just slightly higher than the figure allowed for by the subsidizing organization, based on all their other projects. Every four weeks the project members received four completed week forms from the server with the request to check whether the data was "realistic." If that was not the case for certain items you could make corrections online and in real-time and a new printout was made. After that you signed off four times and you're good to go! Most of the time, all the data was fine. What's more, you could, if you wanted, request a time sheet from the system for the third week in October next year.

Of course, the bureaucrats were fooled, but that was not the aim of the exercise. It was meant to provide maximum time for and focus on the execution of the project for which all researchers were highly motivated. The other day I met one of them and she told me enthusiastically that they had sold the time logging program to another organization that had run into the same problem!

And so we see that it is mainly these "vertical thermometers" that bother the professionals and which management prods and pokes top-down into the primary processes with an increasing appetite and with ever increasing frequency.

The dominant management paradigm: planning & control using vertical rules and procedures

- Procedures for filling out balanced score cards
- Time writing systems
- Presence and absence recordings
- Directives for maintaining holiday cards
- Department budgets and associated release procedures
- Budget realization overview and final calculations
- Obligatory group plans
- Progress report directives
- Subject lists, criteria and forms for functional assessments
- Travel application forms
- Travel claim procedures
- Purchase orders and justification directives
- Rules for visiting conferences, symposia, seminars
- Regulations for receiving and accompanying visitors
- Directives for speaking with the press
- Key procedures
- Signing powers
- Parking (space) regulations
- Ergonomic guidelines and report regulations
- Payroll systems with indications of how they are applied
- Standard figures for the number of books on order and the number of copies, for ink cartridges per full-time equivalent and for printers per square meter
- Standards for the number of secretaries, caterers, etc. per full-time equivalent
- Standards for the number of plant pots, coffee machines and windows per square meter of office space.
- Obligatory template for letters, faxes, reports, slides
- Quality directives, audit commissions, and ISO 9000-circuses
- Procedures for the "emptying of the head" into databases
- Tasks and job descriptions
- Christmas card sending procedures
- Report procedures for this and that
- Customer relationship management directives ("A customer with an annual turnover > $250,000 should, on her or his birthday, be sent a birthday card from the set of approved birthday cards available from Corporate Communications. It is recommended that the message on the card not deviate too much from what is commonly used on such

an occasion. One could think of things such as: 'Warm congratulations on your birthday', or 'Our congratulations and we wish you a pleasant day', or ...").

The incomprehension for this type of frequently infantile bureaucratic "nothingness" can sometimes express itself in extraordinary forms. Recently, I heard a technician say: "We have no budget for this, so it doesn't matter what it costs."

The proliferation of these vertical thermometers is stimulated by the increasing possibilities of IT, pushy consultants or worse still, a combination of both ...

What manager worth his salt can come to his Rotary Club or Lions club without a "management cockpit?" Never before have there been so many cables laid underground, so many antennas put on the roofs, or cameras hung on the walls of our companies. For this reason – with all those sensors – it does not matter anymore where the Corporate HQ is, as long as the manager has his dashboard. Where does this come from? What is the driver? Is it the insecurity of the manager that has not reached the top by climbing up through the ranks and therefore cannot appreciate the intricacies of the business he is in? Has the process become so complex that one man cannot oversee it without the help of these gadgets? Whatever it may be, it happens.

Support comes from an unexpected corner. Thomas Davenport at IBM warns: "Be careful; these systems are less suitable for knowledge professionals. Information technology often makes new process designs possible in operational and administrative areas. The abstract and unstructured inputs to and outputs from knowledge work processes, however, make the application of this technology more difficult. As work becomes more knowledge intensive, rapid manipulation of data across distances has less impact; 'richer,' more face-to-face communications are more important. Technology can support knowledge work processes, but it must be implemented with sensitivity to the nature of the work and its practitioners."

But no one listens, the manager wants or needs his gadget and thus the building of control rooms (in some organizations they even call it the "war room") continues unperturbed. Ideally, a typical "management cockpit" would look as follows: an oval office with at least two rows of monitors showing – in real-time – a balanced scorecard, the share price, production and stock levels, pictures of the shop floor, pictures of meetings-in-progress, where the manager can intervene if things are in danger of moving in the wrong direction (Major Tom to Ground Control), etc. Tom himself sits in his high-tech chair (in which he is able to make long hours) at a moon shaped desk facing the monitors. Sometimes the chair is mounted on a rail so that with one sweep he can slide from one monitor to the next. On his desk are a few remote controls and on his head a headset with microphone.

This description is taken from a visit to a college friend who had become CTO of a listed company. During my (MW) visit he described in great detail his recently "acquired" Control Room, and when I did not quite share his enthusiasm he probably thought that I did not understand so he invited me into his cockpit. After he had demonstrated everything I asked him: "You showed me how you checked what was happening on the shop floor of Hall 4. But perhaps the guys have burned a DVD showing them working hard. They may have put that film on a screen in front of the camera and now they're off playing cards." I was his guest and so I did not want to appear too assertive. "That's possible," said Tom, slightly irritated, "but I don't think so." Since he still didn't seem to understand what I was getting at I pushed a bit further: "You've just bought a new house. Why don't you put the whole shooting match in the living room, that way you wouldn't need to commute to the office anymore?" He apparently found that a better question and there was a moment's silence. Then he said with a smile that he liked "coming home," eager to know what his partner had prepared for dinner; the dog jumping up at him. If you were home all day you would be part of the preparation, which would take away most of the surprise. "Aha, that's what you mean," he said, after the penny had dropped, "whether I interact with workers on the floor?" "Exactly!" I said, and Tom answered that that was rarely the case nowadays because thanks to modern IT that was no longer necessary. "But you're right. Now that you ask me, I really do miss the direct contact with the professionals in the workplace. I think I'll ask my secretary to plan an MBWA (Management By Wandering Around) each Friday from 3 pm onwards."

It will never be the same again between Tom and me. For that he had already taken too high a dose of that MBA stuff.

Another good example is this one:

Lee Iacocca complained about his time with Ford under Henry Ford II, when workforce and management saw each other only every three years when it was time to negotiate a new contract. "And every three years you'd walk into the room with a chip on your shoulder. You wouldn't know the guy and you'd immediately think: I don't like him, he's the enemy. It's like meeting at a bridge and trading spies. You hate the other side, even though the exchange is a good thing."

When at Chrysler as CEO he had learned:

"People that visit my office at Chrysler are often surprised that I do not have a computer terminal on my desk. Maybe they forget that everything that comes out of a computer, someone has to put in. The biggest problem facing American business today is that most managers have too much information. It dazzles them and they don't know what to do with it. The key to success is not information. It's people. The best way to develop ideas is through interaction with fellow managers. This brings us back to the importance of teamwork and interpersonal skills. The chemistry among people sitting together can be incredible and it has been a big part of my success."

In other words, de-bureaucratization is more necessary than ever. If only to create space for the ever-continuing stream of IT-facilitating gadgets, some of which, by directive of the proper authority, will inevitably, unavoidably have to be implemented. That way the number of vertical thermometers may be kept constant. It gives little conciliation, but without continued de-bureaucratization, the amount of thermometers could easily and unnoticeably increase to more than 120% of what the situation was before. Reality is that at all levels new rules are introduced without removing the old ones.

Let us name four (just four) bureaucratization rules of thumb:
1. Does an organization have a planning system without an associated progress-signaling system? If so, that system can be removed!
2. Is there a progress-signaling system without a related planning system? If so, that progress-signaling system can be removed!
3. Are there planning systems that gather data at a different data ag-

gregation level than the associated progress-signaling system (e.g. planning by month and progress signaling in days)? If so, select for both systems the highest of the two aggregation levels.

4. Apply Pareto's Law where ever possible!

Pareto's Law

The quantity of determinant objects in a collection is generally small. Most of these objects are generally relatively unimportant.

Because this statement generally demonstrates an 80/20 pattern, this law is also called the 80/20 rule.

Examples:
- 20% of the employees of a volunteer organization do 80% of the work
- 80% of a manager's problems are caused by 20% of the employees
- 80% of the resistance against change comes from 20% of employees
- 20% of a policy statement contains 80% of the news
- 20% of the vertical rules and procedures can direct or facilitate 80% of the work of professionals. The remaining 20% exceptional cases require 80% rules and procedures.

The recommendation speaks for itself. Put the following question on the agenda of the next management team meeting:

Is it possible and desirable in our situation and based on the 80/20 rule to launch a dramatic de-bureaucratization drive with the following objectives?
- eliminate 80% of the formal systems that plan and check professionals' activities
- simplify by 80% those systems that cannot be eliminated; this should theoretically result in 80% "shorter" forms, procedures and directives
- the resulting freed-up management time must give more attention to the people in the workplace than to the emails and pages with lists, computer outputs, number crunching, planning sheets, adjustments, reviews, progress reports, etc.

If the question about the possibility and desirability of de-bureaucratization is answered positively then it may be interesting to perform the following zero-based experiment:

Think of eliminating all vertical thermometers. Then imagine how the daily work processes would then evolve and what could go wrong. Make a list of problem items and estimate per item the nature and extent of the associated risk. Then think of a – simpler – rule, guideline or procedure for each problem which has a risk that is too large to be controlled by the free play of the professional forces.

In addition to the desire to know constantly the exact current status of things – in other words, the desire to reduce uncertainty – there are a few other important factors in this urge for planning & control (whether automated or not):
- not making real choices or too much "and and" instead of "or or" combined with a
- lack of faith in the involvement and in the self-regulating capacity of the knowledge professionals.

People much rather do things right than wrong

- The entire public sector suffers seriously from bureaucratic money wastage (40% of the Dutch state budget disappears on overheads).
- Judges, teachers, police officers and doctors are, because of the mania for rules, spending more and more time in meetings and on paperwork.
- Consequently they have far less time to do the things they were hired to do.
- We measure and map everything, because politicians cannot make any real choices.
- As a result, the number of (controllers of the) controllers increases all the time.

(Source: Herman Tjeenk Willink, Vice President of the Council of State of the Netherlands, 2005)

Causes:
- half-baked, inconsequential and inconsistent measures (half decentralization; half market effect)
- too many indirect civil servants and support staff: $W_s = f(T_w)$
- lack of trust

Knowledge professionals who, in their private lives make major financial investments, such as buying a house, are somehow assumed to have mislaid this ability when they become part of an organization, and so have to fill out forms to get a new pencil ("Can you please bring the old pencil with you when you come to collect a new one? Can I have a look at it? I'm sorry, but this pencil is not completely used up. I will give you a corporate pencil sharpener; you can use that to sharpen your pencil a few more times, before I give you a new one. Pencils don't grow on trees you know!")

Managers who swear by using planning & control practices from the power model – and that's most of them – have difficulty with the idea that professionals, even at work, much prefer to do something right than do something wrong. I have never met a professional who, as he drives to work, thinks: "let's see what I can mess up today." A knowledge professional who has not been seriously traumatized by previous work experience does not think that sort of thing. In a cookie factory – a metaphor I use for an assembly line with lots of short-cyclical repeated and routine work – things can be somewhat different. Here people are regulated by supply machinery (in, say, chicken slaughter houses or when picking lettuces) or by forms (behind the counters of banks) and I can well imagine that, should the chance arise, they may take the opportunity to throw a spanner in the works of the production process. It provides variety – and an extra coffee break.

That is less likely to happen with knowledge professionals; they have stronger intrinsic motivation and a greater self-regulating capability. That is why a manager who trusts his professionals is not naive. On the other hand, he does need to be watchful that they do not, through sheer enthusiasm, stray from the right track. But this has nothing to do with trust or the need to apply all sorts of "vertical thermometers," but everything to do with collective ambition. And that brings us back to the good news: the energy level of the knowledge professional is a function of their ability to identify with the "values" of the higher goals of the organization. We often call those shared values our mission or, with a less religious connotation, the collective ambition of the organization.

Investing in the shared development of a collective ambition is the other side of the de-bureaucratization coin. Why? Because eliminating vertical rules and procedures leads to greater freedom, more latitude and an increased ability to take control in the workplace.

One would hope that that freedom, that latitude, would be used by knowledge professionals to reach the goals of the organization on time and on budget. That hope is, however, not necessarily justified. Professionals are not by definition the good guys, nor are managers necessarily the bad guys. Knowledge professionals could potentially use this new-found freedom to cut corners or to allow their personal hobbies to occupy more of their time. The chance that this will happen will be less the more professionals feel a greater personal involvement in the higher goals that they strive for together.

The importance of "bonding" professionals with the organization in which they work was also recognized by the researchers Alkahafaji and Tompkins. One of their studies shows a direct and positive relationship between the intensity of the sense of bonding and the level of performance. Provided, of course, that the organization fulfils its function in a dynamic and uncertain environment.

Because professionals in modern organizations generally work in such an environment, a stronger bond with the organization will automatically lead to a higher performance level.

Thus we can conclude that if the organization can maximize the affective bonding with professionals, the energy level of professionals will increase as well as their tendency to internal entrepreneurial behavior. The results of this internal entrepreneurial behavior will generally be in line with the goals the organization wants to reach, because professionals generally feel comfortable in such an environment.

Research by Schmidt and Posner and others shows that the strength of the attraction that a department or an organization exerts on an employee is largely determined by his sense of harmony between personal goals and the collective (higher) goals of the organization. The overlap here represents the shared values. Deal and Kennedy distinguish between *high sharers* and *moderate* and *low sharers*. The personal goals of the first group match most closely with those of the organization: "They are also more likely to feel as if they are an important part of the organization. They are motivated because life at the company has meaning for them."

It is thus extremely important for higher management and most certainly the first-line to invest heavily in the development of a collective ambition. The first-line supervisor can do this together with

the group members by translating the strategy of the next higher ech-
elon in a vision, and deriving from that attainable yet challenging
group targets. The critical success factor here is the level to which
professionals want to commit to the vision and goals. The collective
ambition of the organization should help individual professionals to
develop a personal need to realize the organization's goals. For that, a
minimum requirement is to investigate and define, during the ambi-
tion-development process, the nature and extent of (potential)
shared values and to communicate profoundly – which means deep
and wide – about its meaning.

The bottom line is as follows: the more collective the ambition, the
more shared values, the greater the motivation, the higher the energy
level, the smaller the chance of a "slackers" attitude, the less work
time devoted to hobbies, and the less planning & control is required.
Thus a collective ambition lowers the risk of a drastic de-bureaucratization drive and increases its effectiveness. Couldn't be better!

In this postmodern time, investing in the shared development of a
collective ambition permits the manager still to continue his work in
a more or less traditional way. The postmodern style is typified by
statements such as:
*"You are yourself responsible for your market value. Lifetime em-
ployment no longer exists as we know it. Instead, there is increased emphasis on employability and personal development so that when you
deliver lower added value for our company, you can always find em-
ployment quickly elsewhere. We recognize and understand the natural
mobility of the networking nomads and job hopping is lucrative!"*
    In addition, loyalty and commitment have become old-fashioned
concepts, which is why you'd rather invest in your résumé than in the
company. Here again:
*"No problem, as long as you empty your brains into the database be-
fore you go home at night. Then we can carry on should you decide in the
morning to start your own business or take a survival trip along the
banks of the Amazon River. To avoid misunderstandings, we'd rather
see you stay on for a while since you are still meeting your targets. In
short ,we are happy with you."*
    Meanwhile, the neoclassical style gains further ground. This is

based on the supposition that many people are getting tired of post-modern emptiness. You notice that in the increasing desire to experience emotional events collectively: the funeral of Princess Diana, the NBA play-offs, the rugby world cup, widespread involvement in reality programs such as *Big Brother*, the Olympics madness, mega pop concerts, and so on. In addition, there appears to be an increased need for reflection and spirituality. On every street corner you find New Age meetings, occupancy levels of guest rooms in monasteries in Europe are beating all records.

Big Stories vs. Small Tales ...
The Big Stories are bankrupt, not one single idea (socialism nor liberalism, nor communism, nor capitalism) has led to a fair society. That is why nothing is important any more, and achieving something together is often seen as arrogant. Instead, people start listening more to Small Tales that express hesitant engagement with an ad-hoc ideal. Small Tales like the ones told in an organization by those who have decided to *be* part of the organization.

Shared values generate a synergy-searching collaborative attitude

"The key message to managers of professionals is: create meaning! Help your subordinates find the excitement in their work. Doing this is key for quality and productivity"
(Maister, 1985)

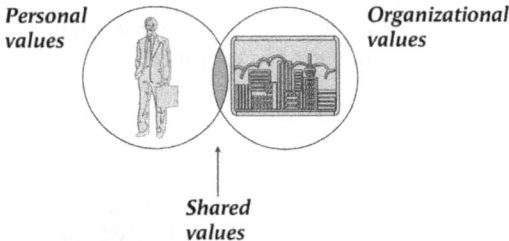

Personal values

Organizational values

Shared values

In the Western world, we live in a well provided and relatively homogeneous society. The primary needs of Maslow are well met for many of us. We have the richest poor and poorest rich and nobody needs to die of cold or hunger. As a result, many are occupied with achieving the higher needs in the Maslow pyramid: belonging, recognition, and self-actualization. Professionals are often amongst those looking for these higher needs. They generally have a good income to satisfy their basic needs and can afford to seek realization of higher immaterial needs. Those needs become "acute" when a professional needs to decide whether he wants to join or stay in an organization. On your way, you meet a group of people who together are doing something to achieve a certain goal or ideal. The (organizational) values of that "club" show so much overlap with your own (personal) values that you decide to become a "member"; you feel the "freedom in bonding." The opposite is also possible; there are so few shared values left between you and all the others in the club that you decide to cancel your membership.

Professionals have a growing need to get a clear answer to the question: Boss, tell me what this is all about? Why are you doing what you do? What is *this organization's reason for existence?* Explain to me why it is worthwhile being here 8 hours a day, 5 days a week, 45 weeks a year, maybe 40 years of my life, in short one third of my total time on Earth. If you deduct sleeping time from the total lifetime of the people in the Western world and you say the result of that is 100%, then you are just shy of spending one third of the time that you are awake running around in some organization or other.

So it makes sense for you to insist that the activities of that organization mean something. Fewer and fewer professionals are prepared to put up with logic such as: "Well, I'm quite prepared to spend that time working so that I can have some extra money that allows me to do what I like in my spare time." No longer do they want to disqualify such a large portion of their time for the sake of a "barter" relationship: "My time for you, your money for me."

Examples of collective ambitions

I will build a car for the great multitude. It will be large enough for the family, but small enough for the individual to run and care for. It will be constructed of the best materials, by the best men to be hired, after the simplest designs that modern engineering can devise. But it will be low in price that no man making a good salary will be unable to own one – and enjoy with his family the blessing of hours of pleasure in God's great open spaces.
Henry Ford

An HR man says to an applicant: "We are trying to provide people with the possibility to enjoy the beautiful countryside with their whole family, which is why we ask you to fit a tiny nipple to a small rod of a tiny shaft 300 times per day. If you do not like that reasoning, because I see you laugh, then it would be better for you to apply for a job with GM down the road. There you have to do the same thing 300 times and yet things are different there because at GM they just make cars!" That's the way it must have been in Detroit in those days.

The day I arrived they had me designing a clutch spring. It had taken me an entire day to make a detailed drawing of it, and I said to myself: "What on earth am I doing? Is this how I want to be spending the rest of my life?"
Lee Iacocca

We believe we will be successful by having the courage to make choices that lead to improving their living environment both inside and outside the company, not by chance but on purpose.
Gerard and Anton Philips

We want to understand and tell everyone how the astonishing diversity of nature has developed; how it works and how it should continue to work on it.
　　We do that for the sake of nature and for humans who are themselves part of it.
Dutch National Natural History Museum, now: Naturalis

We recognize that this is a unique time, when our products will change the way people work and live. It's an adventure and we're in it together.
Apple Inc.

We believe our first responsibility is to the doctors, nurses and patients, to mothers and all others who use our products and services.
　　(NB: Who are not mentioned here? The shareholders, which is exceptional for an American company).
Johnson & Johnson

Light is a visible form of energy,
it pushes back the night,
welcomes the weary,
protects those you love,
banishes monsters from under beds
and makes eyes sparkle.
Philips Lighting

Requirements for an effective collective ambition:

- Collective ambition must express what the professionals want to be for each other and for the society in which they fulfill a function as an organization; what added value they wish to provide.
- Collective ambition must have broad support: by 100% of top-level management and by at least 80% of the remaining employees; collective ambition must be based unconditionally on shared values and standards.
- Collective ambition must give direction toward the desired behavior of the professionals in a way that is inspiring and creates enthusiasm.
- Collective ambition must enable knowledge professionals to provide answers to questions like: Why can I be proud to work here? How do my personal goals match the vision and goals of the organization?
- Collective ambition must be strongly engrained in the procedures for recruitment, selection, assessment and reward.
- The text formulating the collective ambition must abide by the following rules: sentences that start with "we," no clichés and stating the obvious, but passages that appeal and arouse emotion, painting pictures with words. The text should, at the very least, address the following themes: the relevance of the organization to society, the motives of knowledge professionals, and the style of working.

I (MW) once moderated a debate together with Roy Heiner, captain of the team of the Brunel Sunergy sailing boat which achieved very good results in the Whitbread Round the World Race. Roy talked about the depravations which the twelve crew members had suffered: a cycle of four hours sleep and six hours work, with only five sleeping bags and everyone only allowed two pairs of socks and two sets of underwear, because extra weight reduces the speed of the boat. The organizational rules are simple: the individual is there for the team and the team is there to pull off a top-class performance. That is only possible if each member of the team has respect for the professional expertise of the others and if there is an environment of openness in which all knowledge is shared, in order to reach the intended goal more rapidly. Quarrelling is allowed, as long as it is about performing better.

Why is there such a big difference between these two worlds? Does a company or a department operate in so much less an exciting environment than the crew of a racing yacht? Is there not a similar sort of time-based competition? Why does it take so much effort in organizations to recognize synergy and start cooperating and helping each other? The answer is pure and simple: lack of collective ambition. There are too many sub-interests, there is too much competition and territorial instinct with too many mini kingdoms, there is too much political maneuvering ...

Professionals in a mission-driven organization instinctively tend to tailor their energy and talents to those of their colleagues. This will increase the likelihood of achieving the collective ambition. Wherever personal goals and organizational ambitions largely overlap, there is no room for the hobbyist or soloist. Moreover, the required synergies will automatically be the most effective, because the search motive is driven by the need of reaching common higher goals that fit the organization's raison d'être.

An enlightened manager at Shell Global Solutions once said: "We concentrate more on shared values and therefore more on culture than on rules and procedures. Family feeling, team spirit and *esprit de corps*, that's what it is about, although we must always watch out that it does not become too elitist. It is most important that you feel at home here and that your surroundings give you a feeling that you can develop your talents for many years to come. We believe in on-the-job learning, we invest a lot in learning opportunities and giving people continuing opportunities to improve and renew their competencies. If someone were to tell me or a colleague that although he is still inspired by my vision and our collective ambition and still finds us a splendid group of people, he nevertheless wants to quit because he can no longer learn enough here, then we have failed miserably. If for that reason the commitment and the allegiance of the professionals are put under pressure, then we fail collectively."

"A fantastic story," you may say, "but not everyone has the privilege of belonging to that subtly operating and existentially reflecting group of knowledge professionals that you like to talk about so much. Currently you also have 60% of the working population without a degree in their

back pocket, all doing their bit and for the most part cheerfully. What good is this kind of talk to them?"

The honest answer is: not much, although the group mentioned is rapidly becoming smaller. That is because a lot of physical work can be automated, or is transferred to low-wage countries. Granted, in call centers (the sweat shops of the knowledge economy; it does not smell of sweat but the working conditions are similar), in the hotel and catering industry, at cookie factories, and at all those other organizations where people literally or figuratively have "to fit a tiny nipple to a little shaft using a small screw" 300 times per day, you will not get far with stories about shared values and collective ambitions. "Precisely! They are only too glad to escape from that misery at 5 pm sharp. When they finally get home, there are other ambitions like tending the garden, playing in a band, sitting on committees, building violins, photographing insects, repairing old clocks, acting, model trains, giving Kung Fu lessons, you name it."

Logically enough: if, in your job, you are reduced to a voice that reads out pre-scripted narratives or to hands that can cut, turn and squeeze, sort, put together, and so on, then there is no room for self actualization. The only opportunity for capitalizing on your talents is "outside" the organization. Professionals must be able to have that room inside the organization, otherwise they would not be there, because they *are* the organization.

Get high on your own supply!

Some time ago I (MW) moderated a management team meeting that had retreated for two days to the countryside in order to define a long-term vision and collective ambition for their business unit. During a discussion about the involvement and family feeling of the staff, one of the participants spoke about something that had occurred in his previous job. A supervisor of an assembly line in a TV factory that handled the assembly of Philips TV sets had a Sony TV in his own home. He said a Sony TV was "far better" than a Philips TV set. He didn't say that after work he wanted to escape from the Philips world where he spent each and every day. Nor did he say that the components of the one TV were much better or the whole thing was slightly better than the other. No, it was "far better." The Consumer's Guide knew better.

Not a single employee at the Trabant car factory in the former East Germany will be blamed for honestly admitting that he prefers a Mercedes or an Audi to a Trabant. But someone who day in day out makes TV sets that are no different in quality from the ones by the competition and nevertheless prefers a product from the very company with which his own company is in fierce competition, is acting a bit strange.

Ergo: people who feel little attachment to the organization where they work, who squander their energy from 8 to 5 simply for the money they receive in return, are throwing away a large part of their lives.

If you do not feel involved in your work, be brave and break out of the rut and look for a company where you do feel at home.

Managers are frequently blamed for not having higher goals or a vision. That may be so in a number of cases. On the other hand, it is near impossible to share a vision with the above mentioned supervisor.

"The key message to managers of professionals is: create meaning! Help your subordinates to find the excitement in their work. Doing this is the key to quality and productivity." We now understand this beautiful statement from David Maister and we agree with it. If that is not the case, then you'd better put this book aside and go play golf or any other expensive form of walking.

The beauty of what Maister is saying is that in the case of a collective ambition, you are really not bothered by Mintzberg's observation that professionals cannot be managed by imposing rules and procedures or by imposing information systems. Because why would you cut corners, why would you be lazy when you are achieving your own goals and *en passant* those of the organization and vice versa? That is not logical. In strong ideology-driven organizations like Amnesty International, Doctors Without Borders, The Body Shop, Brazil's Semco, (but also Al Qaeda) you see that vertical rules and procedures hardly play a role.

A "Doctor Without Borders" does not need to have a yearly performance assessment with the head of Borders telling him: "My friend, I have here a timesheet from Rwanda for Thursday 14 October and I see that on that day you did not make your first incision until 8:20 am instead of 8 am, as we agreed. Why was that?" That would be nonsense because as a Western doctor you have given up quite a bit to exercise your profession in the harsh conditions customary to Doctors Without Borders. An operative of Greenpeace does not call his boss and says: "Boss it is five o'clock. I have been sitting on this chimney for eight hours, where is my relief!" That is also nonsense. You want to finish the job, because you elected to do it because you believe in it.

Berlin philosopher Wilhelm Schmid (2001) gives a broader perspective to the match between personal and organizational goals by classifying "work for bread" as just one of many forms of work that determine that feeling of leading a meaningful life.

The *éminence grise* of European organizational science Charles Handy* agrees: "And yet I have the feeling that there are more and more people who want to give more content to their lives. If an organization wants to keep its good employees, it becomes its responsibility to provide a higher goal. If you want to retain talent you have to formulate an ideal. Otherwise you get a purely instrumental relationship in which I only work for you to make money. Or because by doing so I can acquire skills that I can use elsewhere. That leads to egoistic short-term thinking. I believe that the most beautiful and most satisfying thing in life is to have a goal that rises above oneself. If the goal only worries you, it will evaporate quickly. To open a bottle of wine all for yourself is perhaps nice for the first glass, but after the fourth glass the feeling is a lot less nice. No one to talk to. No one to share things with. If you do not have a goal outside yourself, larger than yourself, you will ultimately be disappointed. I therefore believe that the focus that companies have right now – to be an instrument to increase the wealth of the owners with the help of the labor of the workers – needs to shift to: a society with an ideal."

In the early nineties Philips Electronics ran a large scale organization change program called "Operation Centurion." The main aim was to change the self-centered "inward looking culture" of The Great Dutch Debating Club and to achieve a dramatic productivity improvement by getting at least the same turnover with 40,000 fewer people. At the time of that transformation, which shook the organization to its foundations, I (MW) worked as a consultant at Corporate O&E (Organization and Efficiency), a group of advisers to the Board with people such as C.K. Prahalad, Sumantra Ghoshal and Vijay Sathe, the main contractors of the Centurion process. Needless to say, I learned a lot!

It was the consultants' opinion that a successful organization is

* In: R. Gibson: *Rethinking the Future,* 1997

characterized by an explicit collective (= broadly carried) ambition and by targeted alignment of knowledge and other capabilities that are necessary to realize that ambition.

Their diagnosis was that Philips was at that time in the "*quiet strength quadrant*" (see the figure hereafter). There was a lot of knowledge and capacity, but where was the target? Depending on the random outcome of an interaction of forces, the organization swung strategically from left to right: in and out of software, in and out of telephones, in and out of the media business, in and out of medical systems, etc.

Additionally, there is the "*fantasy position*" in which the collective ambition is totally clear, but the organization cannot mobilize the knowledge and the other resources to realize that ambition. In this quadrant, we find many political organizations and organizations that generate texts (they, of course, call that "policy making").

Then there is the "*peace and quiet*" area where you cannot do much together, but that isn't so bad because you really don't want to do much anyway. And finally there is the "*succes*" area that obviously does not require further explanation.

The position of our Indian friends was that if an organization is somewhere in the central area and is looking for the way to success, the chance for success is larger if an investment is first made in developing and clarifying the collective ambition. The resources for achieving that ambition will appear almost by themselves, because

Capacity as a function of ambition

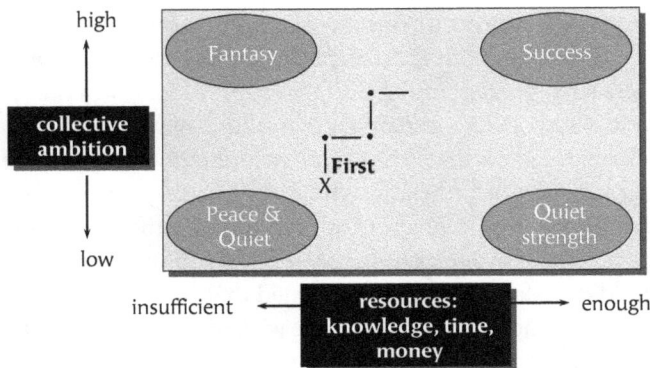

"where there is a will, there is always a way." So do not play the record that is still played in many public companies: "Yes, but if we all want to do that, we *first* need more money, more people and more policy." Those who think this way would do better to consult Nietzsche – a recognized source when it comes to defining collective ambitions – who once said: "He who has the *why*, can answer to almost every *how*."

This was an example of a company that formulated an ideal. Let me (CH) give you a real-life example of how other multinationals go about "inspiring" people in the wrong way.

When I started working for Shell in the mid-1970s as a young engineer, there only seemed to be one ambition that we all had in common: quickly get a foot on the management ladder. Knowledge and the development of professional skills were merely instruments for reaching that objective. It was all about job categories, helicopter view, marked leadership, scoring points, and current estimate potentials. We all agreed that Shell, with its sophisticated and intensive in-house training program, provided an ideal platform to get ahead in the oil and gas industry. But I never heard someone say they wanted to become the best reservoir engineer or drilling engineer because there was no future in specialization. Hence, there was no stimulus in that direction either. The only time during my entire involvement with Shell (joining and leaving several times and working in the intervening periods as a consultant) that I heard something approaching a common company ideal was when I heard the CEO tell an audience of employees in Melbourne, Australia, in 1997 that he wanted to raise ROACE (Return on Average Capital Employed) from 8% to 10%. And asked about his ideal organization he answered "Pepsi Cola." Guess why: because of Pepsi's 12% ROACE! That was the vision he shared with us. The remainder was about market analyses and share prices. Needless to say, he was an accountant. It was very disappointing for me not to hear anything about the great business we were in, the beauty of it, or about appreciation for the very people he was addressing. No one even asked about these things and, to my shame, I didn't dare ask either. It seemed that in 20 years, Shell was still a people-grinding money machine with nothing more to offer to its workforce than financial reward and the top-level management carrot. In 2005, when I got back with them at their head office in The Hague I still did not see any change. Young engineers were still given the same perspective as thirty years before. The consequence is that personnel turnover is ever increasing, because engineers are in a way more mature, and are looking for more in their professional life than working in faraway exotic places on good salaries with unrealistic career prospects and a good pension, but no job satisfaction. Good engineers and geologists are pulled out of their specialty and pushed into management positions because it is the only promotion path that remains above the first-line manager's position. This often creates a lose/lose situation for both the specialist and for Shell. The first ends up unhappy in his job while the latter ends up with de-motivated and uninspired managers. Fortunately for Shell, the profit margins in oil and gas exploration and production have allowed this to continue and function for years. If Shell had produced cars it would not have stayed in business for long. My diagnosis? Like Philips, Shell sits firmly in the quiet strength quadrant. Because of its much more competitive environment, Philips had to do something, Shell did not. Thus far ...

The magic effect of a collective ambition does not apply to organizations that are similar to a cookie factory. Here people cannot influence the quality and speed of their work and you can apply vertical planning and rules because head and hands have to follow machines, screens or forms (Counter No.1: "You can't get a work permit if you don't have a resident's permit," Counter No. 2: "You can't get a resident's permit if you don't have a work permit.") These are environments in which work processes are deterministic because there is a high degree of certainty about relationships between input and output. For most knowledge-intensive organizations, however, there is no such certainty. As said before: a judge cannot guarantee that the criminal – after sitting out his sentence – will not commit a crime again. Management consultants cannot promise a company that profits will soar after implementing their advice. A patient operated on completely according to the rules, can relapse next week.

In short: knowledge-intensive organizations are working in an area where certainty about causalities in the primary process is restricted. Stacey – who sees organizations as "Complex Adaptive Systems" – divides that area into two areas: the zone of complexity and the political arena where chaos thrives. The relationships that we have tried to explain here are illustrated in the diagram below. From it, one can see how a knowledge-intensive organization that invests in the development of shared values can move away from the areas where chaos reigns and political behavior sets the tone.

When to focus management more on collective ambition than on rules and procedures?

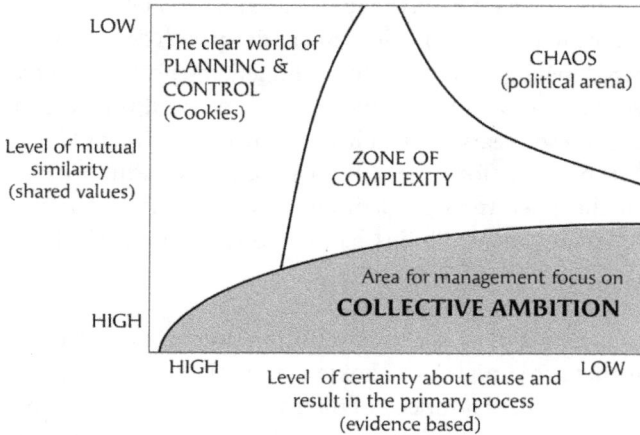

Summary statement:
Without collective ambition based on shared values, the organization will eventually become an archipelago where bureaucracy thrives and where there is no passion.

There are only two basic motives why people work together:
1. because they have to (if you do not stick to the vertical rules and procedures, you get fired), or
2. because they want to, inspired by a collective ambition.

Two summarized recommendations for those who manage professionals:
a) Be very aware of the effect and thus the importance of planning & control. Awareness is the driver behind de-bureaucratization.

b) Parallel to that, invest in participative development (and continuous actualization) of the collective ambition. Trust the knowledge, loyalty, and self-regulating capacity of the professionals. Give them room to maneuver and the regulating facility to act accordingly.

We end this chapter with a romantic quote from French writer Antoine de Saint-Exupery:

If you want to build a ship,
don't drum up people to collect wood
and don't assign them tasks and work,
but rather teach them to long for the endless immensity of the sea.

A vertical and a diagonal method for developing a collective ambition

The type of collective ambition that we support is based on extensive participation of employees during the gestation process. Extensive participation is vital because what really counts for knowledge-intensive organizations is acceptance by the complete workforce of (management) decisions. The closer the workers are involved in the decision-making process the better it is.

According to Moss Kanter (1985), this kind of involvement implies intensive two-way communication as a minimum requirement. "Behind the rise of participative management today is the notion that *ownership* counts in getting commitment to actions, that if people are given a say in decisions, they feel better about them."

In this addendum we review two methods to arrive at an effective collective ambition:
1. a vertical method and
2. a diagonal method.

Both typically contain a high level of participation by both managers and the knowledge workforce. In the vertical method there is a more top-down approach, whereas in the diagonal method it is more bottom-up.

The vertical method
For a description of the vertical method we use the Scientific Education Institution as an example. For the consultant – who plays an important role in this procedure – we can use either an external or an internal (HR) consultant. The most important criterion for the choice of consultant is that he or she is capable and prepared to assume a facilitating attitude as well as an interested (and not self-interested) position.

Phase 1: Interviews with direct questioning
The consultant conducts two to four interviews with the Board, asking questions such as:
- Why is it important that the institute exists and continues to exist?
- What can the employees be proud of?
- What distinguishes the institute from other similar institutes?
- What drives each of you to give leadership to the institute?
- Is there a "we feeling" or a feeling of *esprit de corps*?
- If so: how does it manifest itself?
- If not: why not?
- What is so good about your organization?

After the first interview the advisor draws up the first version of the collective ambition. This should be no longer than one page and is used in the second interview.

Now the second round of questions begins:
- Is this an accurate description?
- What precisely do you mean by that word or paragraph?
- Could there be groups in the institute that think differently about this subject?
- If so: why do you think that is the case?
- It is my impression that you prefer to keep this vague.
- Is that so and if so why do you want that?

Based on the results of this interview the consultant will write a second version of the collective ambition.

Depending on the speed with which growing consensus is achieved, this process can be repeated once or twice, in turn leading to a third and fourth version. The more advanced the version, the more the writing of the developing collective ambition shifts from the consultant to the board members.

Phase 2: Interviews with indirect questioning
The working method in the second phase is identical to that of the first phase, but now we use analogies to try to uncover implicit unconscious opinions. Here, the following types of questions are pertinent:

If you were asked to compare your institute to an animal, or a color, or a sport, or a car, a musical instrument, an orchestra, what would be your response and why?

Once again, there are follow-up interviews and one or two repetitions, resulting in versions five and six.

Phase 3: Informal broadening and deepening
The board members carry the last version for a fixed period (say one month) with them in their briefcase. They are asked to discuss it – or fragments of it – ad hoc with employees they meet in their daily work (before or after meetings, in the corridors, during cocktails). They should ask questions like: What do you think of this? Does this reflect what we are? Is there something missing? Does this reflect who we are? The results of these informal reviews are processed in the next version of the collective ambition.

Phase 4: Formal broadening and deepening
In this phase we set up debating sessions in which a board member of the full board clarifies the latest version of the collective ambition with the aim of getting feedback from the participants. These meetings can be organized both vertically (for one faculty, for support staff) and horizontally (for all the faculty boards, for all teaching heads).

Phase 5: Finalization of the collective ambition and ongoing interpretation
Finally the board draws up the definitive text of the collective ambition, after which it can be introduced. This guarantees at the very least continuing communication (in policy notes, during internal training sessions, in annual addresses) and interpretation of the collective ambition to guide certain decision-making processes, for instance in recruiting people, in doing business with certain suppliers or countries and foremost in the cooperative attitude between managers and employees. Also the collective ambition can be the starting point for (re)formulating the vision, the goals and the strategy of the institute.

The "vertical method" described here can take six to nine months, during which one can go easily through ten or fifteen versions of the collective ambition, before there is sufficient consensus and everyone has a good feeling about the latest draft.

As said before, it is mainly about the process in which everyone together is searching for shared values. The wish to have one sheet of paper with a text is in the end only an alibi to get the process going. As soon as there is clarity about the raison d'être and the shared values of the organization, that sheet of paper can go into the waste basket.

The diagonal method

The heart of the diagonal method is a large-scale seminar. As an example, we take a research institute: RI. The research directors function as the client of the consultant, who directs and moderates the seminar. In preparation there is a pre-investigation.

Seminar The consultant, together with the research directors, sets up a seminar forum that consists of between thirty and one hundred participants. A forum much smaller than thirty people will marginalize the base support for the seminar's outcome. With a forum larger than one hundred it becomes difficult to have meaningful discussions in the plenary sessions and it decreases the chance of recycling opinions and proposals from the sub-groups. What is essential is that the forum represents a cross section of the primary process of the research institute (no support staff). For a research institute, the forum may consist of three directors, all (ten) group leaders plus a further five employees from each research group – to be selected by the group leader – preferably high potentials. This results in a forum size of 63 people. A second condition is that the forum is new in its composition, because only then can you break through the meeting and decision-making culture everyone is accustomed to in formal board meetings, group leader gatherings, etc. Managers who have been part of those formal meeting groups have, over the years, become used to each other's mannerisms. Cross compositions revitalize a certain alertness that has been pushed to the background.

The aim of the seminar is to arrive at a broadly supported and appealing wording of the collective ambition. Hence, during the various day seminars, a number of group tasks are carried out in sub-groups of varying composition. The cumulative output of the preceding group task will be the input for the following task. Thus a time concentrated process can take place, whereby ever-improving versions of the draft collective ambition finally converge into a text to be included in the final declaration of the seminar. The results of the pre-investigation (see below) are included in the group tasks and the same subjects are addressed as mentioned in phase 1 and 2 of the vertical method.

Pre-investigation The pre-investigation to prepare for the seminar has three purposes:
1. To enable a flying start
2. To raise awareness of what is about to happen and
3. To involve the people who are not in the forum in the process.
This investigation consists of individual and roundtable interviews on the following subject:

Potential shared values and desired forms of behavior that are considered representative for the institute.

A shared value often takes the form of a statement (e.g. the streets in town must be safe, or, there's always money available for a good project). The wording of desired behavior mostly starts with "we" (we do not exceed 30 miles an hour in town, we stimulate internal entrepreneurship). A guideline for the number of interviews is two times the amount of forum members.

Examples of the kinds of questions asked:
• Consider researchers that have become group leaders in the recent time: which standards of behavior do they have in common?
• With what should the professionals identify themselves: with their profession, with their research group, or with their institute?
• What form does that identification really take?
• Tell us an anecdote or personal experience that is typical of the culture, the way you interact at the institute.
• Name one subject not related to a discipline in which the institute is better than any competitor. Name one thing not related to a discipline that the institute must stop tomorrow (if that is possible).

Finally, the outcome is analyzed and the results are presented in a findings report that is explained at the beginning of the seminar and that will be the subject of the first sub-group's task. With the help of the findings, part of that task will be how to create building stones or fragments that can be used in the collective ambition of the institute. This process then culminates in determining the definitive text of the collective ambition followed by its introduction in the way described in phase 5 of the vertical method.

Focus points
We would like to end this summary of the two methods with three important focus points:

- The influence and involvement of top-level management must be high. If the highest-level leaders do not believe in a collective ambition, effectiveness will be marginal, because the most important tasks of top-level management will be to continuously exemplify and reinforce that what the organization stands for.
- It is recommended only to lift the draft status of the collective ambition at the very last moment. It is a fact – based on experience – that as long as the document is called a draft, professionals are prepared to continue to pay attention and energy to a subject that is generally considered vague.
- When using the collective ambition, it will become ever clearer which sentences of the statement are most relevant in everyday practice. Hence, contrary to many other policy documents, the collective ambition is a living document that can be compacted and re-formulated the more it is used and understood.

2 STRATEGY

The strategy is: Innovation and operational excellence and customer focus

Why waste more and more time, energy and brain power writing fat reports full of strategic analyses and plans? Opportunities and threats have already gone stale before we have even had a chance to determine the strategic issues, even after extensive soul searching of our formal classification of strengths and weaknesses. Strategic Planning Departments, with their parameters, benchmarks and trend developments that form the basis for recommending a strategy, serve no purpose.

These are the kind of suggestive statements that find their justification in the dynamics and turbulence of what Castells called the "Casino Society" of which we have all become a part. If you want reports: invest in writing strategic scenarios.

Enter the collective ambition.

From the collective ambition we first derive what knowledge, or what level of perfection is necessary to realize that ambition with sufficient chance of success. Then an assessment is made of where, in which of the required knowledge areas, breakthroughs can be expected and what these will look like; not only technological, but also economical, ecological, political and sociocultural breakthroughs. Based on that, we can then define possible to probable future scenarios that need such knowledge to realize the collective ambition.

The dynamics in the Global Casino are the reason why we know less and less precisely which buttons to press and in what order to achieve the desired effect tomorrow. No more "dashboards." If a prospective course is clear, we know from the outset that that clarity will be only short-lived. Ever-changing coalitions and spontaneous networking increasingly introduce new goals and strategies, with continuously shifting forces. There are hardly any safe refuges left.

Globalization of the playing field is also why demographical, (macro)-economical, sociocultural, technological, ecological and political developments follow each other in quick succession with the technological breakthroughs functioning as the catalysts.

Look at the progress and changes in transportation technology (Airbus and Boeing), nano and megatronics, information and communication systems (internet), biotechnology, etc. Things also changed in the old days but the influence of such changes was mainly restricted to the local cultures from which they originated. As a result, the rate at which changes took place was slower than now. Changes in one country did not cause immediate changes in others. Now that everything is interconnected and everyone communicates with everyone else, the change frequency in the Global Casino is the sum of all these local changes. Everyone in *advanced economies* is occupied with innovation, knowing that a successful innovation, can, at least for some time, have a worldwide impact and as such yield considerable profit. The number of questions and problems that can be posed from whatever disciplinary angle is almost unlimited. As are the criteria that the related innovative ideas, answers and solutions according to numerous stakeholders and interested parties must fulfill.

Against that background it is not strange to see that the time span between setting fixed strategic plans (if any) has become shorter. Gone are the days when it was important to think in terms of a long-term strategy with substantiated choices applicable for the next four or five years. The period during which the modern knowledge-intensive organization can work undisturbed on the realization of the determined strategy is barely longer than the time it takes to develop that strategy.

From up close, the current necessary linking of short-cyclic strategy determining processes looks like a constant flow of strategic decisions. It is now a continuous process, the only constant being nonstop strategic reorientation, with the collective ambition as the resilient frame of reference.

Given the developments outlined above, it is naïve to expect anything further from traditional strategic SWOT exercises and Porterian OR-OR analyses. "The stone age did not end due to lack of stones," said Michiel Groeneveld, research manager at Shell. Because of the strongly increased magnification of scale, dynamics and complexity of the atmosphere in which the professional has to operate, we find ourselves in the middle of a mine field. More than before, quicker action is required with much more uncertainty and ambiguity. Uncertainty because the available time to gather and analyze information has become less. That ambiguity is threefold:

1. Ambiguity of understanding: where people have different views on the situation, give different interpretations of mutually experienced phenomena and tell different stories about the same thing.
2. Ambiguity of intention: that can be rather obstructive in developing a collective ambition; people do not know what they want, or do not agree, or say one thing and do another.
3. Ambiguity of participation: the composition of the groups involved varies continuously because of changing coalitions and ambitions, managers that take on another challenge, job-hopping professionals, and so on.

The perplexities, contradictions and paradoxes that arise as a result do not go well with the rational analytical nature of traditional methods and techniques for determining strategy. We now live in an AND-AND time. The modern customer wants products and services that are available, cheap and innovative, and precisely fit their individual needs. Knowledge-intensive organizations no longer have markets, instead they have customers with a name.

Is there safe refuge left? Yes, there are in fact two: generic strategy and intuition.

We will discuss intuition later. The generic strategy is the same for every knowledge-intensive organization. The level of perfection with which we execute a strategy determines our competitive position. According to Treacy & Wiersema, a generic strategy is based on the following logical as well as plausible concepts. If the collective ambition matches the strategy – depending on what is central in the organization: product innovation, process innovation, or service innovation – there are only three factors that are simultaneously and continuously important: customer orientation (customer intimacy), efficiency (operational excellence) and innovation (product, technological, or service leadership).

Generic strategy for a knowledge-intensive organization

- *Innovation: Product, Technological, or Service Leadership:*
Focus on continued renewal of products, processes, or services, based on state-of-the-art knowledge and technology (me-first; management of opportunities; in terms of Porter: differential strategy)
Necessary: innovation management and knowledge management

- *Efficiency: Operational Excellence:*
Focus on marketing a balanced range of products or services that stand out because of their optimum price-quality ratio (me-too; management of operations; in terms of Porter: cost-leadership strategy)
Necessary: quality management and process and chain management

- *Customer Intimacy:*
Focus on offering integrated, complete solutions (tailor-made and turn-key) to fulfill the needs of well-defined groups of customers.
Necessary: alliance management and project/program management

The guiding principle behind this strategy theory can be explained as follows:

If the organization scores at least a four out of five on each of its three critical strategic factors, and if it is clear on which of the three factors should be economized last when resources get scarce, then that organization is indestructible.

Hence, the strategic analysis can be simple, costs little time and is not expensive because it can be done without the help of consultants. Ask as many professionals as possible in the primary process to score intuitively each of the three factors. If the number of professionals is large enough the average scores should be meaningful. That should give us the factor that needs to be worked on most to get the score to or above four.

Next, present the relevant management teams the following case. "Colleagues, imagine our company (division, practice area, department) hits on hard times and there is hardly any money left for internal investments, to be precise, only 100,000 dollars. We must decide on the three proposals that are now on the table. One to improve on Operational Excellence, one to improve on Customer Intimacy and one to improve on Product/Technology/Service Leadership. The investment that is available for each of the proposals is exactly 100,000 dollars. Each of the proposals can only be implemented in full; none can be done by half. These are packaged deals and the quality of each of the proposals is of a comparable level.

With a gun to your head, the question now is: to which proposal shall we commit our last 100,000 dollars?"

According to the 80/20 rule of Pareto, at least 80% of the participants should give the same answer. If not, that would mean a lack of clear strategic choices and we would have to be extremely worried about the company's future. In summary: make sure that for all three you score a four or more and know which factor has priority when resources are scarce. And there is a strategy you can work with and only marginal measuring is required to steer things in the right direction. Modern knowledge-intensive organizations only need to monitor four performance criteria; all concern "time," because "time is money."

1. Time-to-Market

Are we on time with our new products, i.e. are we beating our competition to the market? Are we able to capitalize on the "first mover" advantage? You win if you hit the market with an innovative product that has about the same price as the product that it replaces.

Knowledge-intensive organizations that have opted for a hyper-competitive strategy*, introduce all-new replacement products and services to the market before the life cycle of their existing products has reached the highest point on the S curve. Examples of such companies are: Apple, Audi, Intel, Nokia, Sony but also hospitals, digital services providers and software developers. They do not wait until the competitive lead for a particular product has reached the maximum return on investment. They even hurt themselves by bringing yet another product generation or service on the market at the moment that fast followers are about to introduce comparable product-market combinations. That way it eventually becomes too expensive for the competition to keep up with those continuously innovating me-first companies. A company that does this all the time can truly claim to be "too-fast-to follow."

---

*   For more information see: D'Aveni, 1994

Company gatekeepers are generally experienced professionals with a special interest in a particular competitor. Because they once worked there (internship, promotion research), because they admire the technical achievement of that company or because they speak the language of the country that the company is from (e.g. Japan).

From his company's strategic perspective, the company gatekeeper routinely collects relevant information about his target company: annual reports, internet info, articles in the financial press, especially about strategic alliances and other cooperative initiatives. The gatekeeper reflects, makes links and presumes strategic developments. He gives an internal seminar on his findings twice a year.

For instance, an industrial research laboratory, IRL, has a company gatekeeper for each of their most important competitors. A researcher from the IRL can only travel to (an alliance partner of) one of those four companies if the gatekeeper signs off on the travel request form. The traveler must visit the gatekeeper prior to his trip and the gatekeeper can ask him to pay attention to certain aspects or to ask certain questions. Normally, these are things that the traveler would never think of because they are not the reason for his visit. "We suspect that they want to apply technology T to improve process P. If that is so, they must have built a site O near a lake or a river. Could you pay attention to that and if you get a chance ask about it in a roundabout way?" The travel expense claim must also be signed off by the gatekeeper to make sure that the debrief is not forgotten.

2. Time-to-Money

How fast is the return investment? This performance criterion is important because as a result of faster innovations, product life cycles are shorter. That means that new money must be constantly (and faster) available to develop new products.

3. Time-to-Competence or Time-to-Volume

How fast can the company mass produce new products from prototype and pilot production? Or how long does it take to make 30 advisors available when at the moment there are only 3? Here it is about the speed with which certain internal knowledge can be "multiplied." This performance criterion has been introduced by Lew Platt, the former CEO of Hewlett Packard who gave his annual speech the title: "If we only knew what we know!"

4. Time-to-Get-Connected

How fast can we connect with external partners who have complementary skills to give customers the turnkey solutions that they want or need? Knowledge-intensive organizations that are very enthusiastic about this performance criterion often call themselves "solutions integrator" or something similar. What is relevant here are the alliance skills of the company, the ability to accomplish profitable cooperation efficiently. Time-to-Get-Connected has become so important because it has become an illusion to think that in today's Casino Society it is still possible to stay ahead of the competition by creating – as Porter describes it – a sustainable competitive edge. Such a form of sustainability has become extremely rare. Instead of trying to avoid the competition, you should *seek out* the competition by participating with it in ever-changing networks. In these networks, a short-lived advantage can be obtained over those that are not part of these networks.

Strategic Homework I: Call yourself creative, capitalize on your undoubted experience with the balanced scorecard, and find procedures to measure each of the aforementioned "time-to" criteria in your own organization. Design requirements: simple, elegant, and free of bureaucracy.

It would be nice if together with the introduction of new "time-to" measuring, you can announce the removal of at least four of the existing "vertical thermometers."

Strategic Homework II: None of the four "time-to" performance criteria can be coupled exclusively to any of the three strategic success factors. Each score on the four criteria specifies more or less the level of innovation, the operational excellence and the customer orientation. Draw the 4x4 matrix and fill out the cells for the current and for the desired situation in your organization, division, practice area, department, or project.

One collective ambition, three generic strategy success factors and four time-to performance criteria. That is all it takes for a modern knowledge-intensive organization to get going.

This chapter continues with some reflections regarding the remaining success factor: **customer intimacy or customer orientation.**

When we talk about customer orientation, the first question that should arise must be: is there an alternative? We think not! Even in a situation where the interaction between customer and supplier is relatively binding, they talk about jail birds. And if you can't make it pleasant you must still try to make it easier. It's a matter of respect. Discussions about supply-driven versus demand-driven distort the issue. The Global Casino has been individualized and even partly atomized and hence all analogue and digital transactions with stakeholders are driven by dialogue. In case we need more differentiation because otherwise things get too "gray," one can always use the following rule of thumb: where there is a large difference in expertise between customers and suppliers, it is better to work supply-driven than demand-driven. Especially because the customer lacks the expertise to know what he can demand. All music lovers wanted to have better needles in the tonearms of their record player that would reduce noise and crackle when playing a record. None of them said: "Stop that mechanical nonsense with needles, it will never amount to anything. Go record music with light, digitize music first, burn the codes in little dots on a plate and read them with a small laser beam, preferably in blue because blue light has a shorter wavelength so you can get more dots on a plate!"

If the difference in expertise is small – as in many business-to-business situations – then it is better to work more demand-driven. That way nurses working in "care" can work more demand-driven than the specialists who are dealing with "cure." For a nurse it is less productive to ask the patient what he wants to eat the evening before the operation, whether he wants local anesthetic or whether he wants a spare set of blood bags on stand-by in case he loses too much blood.

Ton de Leeuw, an MBA professor at Groningen University, once explained it very clearly: "The whole debate about demand-driven versus supply-driven versus dialogue-driven is, to a large extent, about semantics. You just have to work precisely." That is the essence of customer orientation: simply do your job properly and every professional feels intuitively when he does not.

Apart from managing the tension between supply and demand driven, "Working Precisely" demands addressing a second polarity:

creating a workable balance between distance and involvement. That is easier said than done. It is about attitude, a disposition that is different for each customer and that can change for the same customer over time. Disposition goes with empathy, presence (be there) and attentively listening and communicating in a language the customer understands. Involvement is also about taking the customer seriously and not pushing one's own learning and developing targets. ("Great, this gives a good opportunity to experiment with the new XYZ method; maybe from a client's perspective it is a bit like shooting a cannon at a fly, but it will solve his problem and in turn I can learn. You know what? I will turn it into a lead customer approach project.")

Distance means assertiveness, saying exactly how it is. That in turn means avoiding soft behavior and being super-pleasing: no desserts, no compromising on the service quality for the sake of approval. Distance is also about not doing what you cannot do. That demands daring and wanting to refer to colleagues and that is difficult for two reasons. One, you don't make any money and two, you admit there is something you cannot do. Unfortunately, it is still the case in many disciplines that acknowledging your own weaknesses does not gain much respect.

Building a broad interaction repertoire and always selecting the right mix of distance and involvement is the art of the professional. Add know-how and the mix would be perfect. This particularly applies to professionals in the service industry who have direct contact with the customers – doctors, lawyers, accountants, architects, advisors, etc. – and much less to professionals who are each other's clients such as those in research institutes, R&D departments and in business-to-business projects. If you find it difficult to learn the necessary variety in interaction, look for the solution on the other side. Homogenize the customer group that you want to work for to your favorite form of interaction.

You may have noticed from this that for a knowledge worker, at least two forms of specialization are important: a technical-substantive specialization in the discipline and a process specialization toward style of interaction.

We visualize the two-by-two matrix: narrow and broad interaction

repertoires versus narrow and broad specializations and we can proba-
bly see the quadrant where we can place the "nerd."

Based on interaction considerations, the narrower the selected market segmentation, the larger the danger of pigeon-holing. The tendency of professionals is to define customer problems in terms of solutions that *they* can offer. You see application opportunities for what you are good at. You sell mutton as lamb. Based on interactive motives or discipline considerations, the smaller the market segment, the bigger the inclination to force the problem of the client into a known pattern. Experience has taught us that the chance of pigeon-holing decreases the more the professional can muster respect for the (added) values of those disciplines that are not his or her own. Discipline-exceeding information and exchange meetings foster the development of that respect and increase the chance of productive multidisciplinary and interdisciplinary cooperation.

"Of course we are customer oriented!"

A management consultancy performed a research study into the functioning of a company engaged in business services. The consultancy observed that the biggest shortcoming was a lack of customer orientation. The management disagreed. No matter how hard the consultancy tried to convince them, the company insisted that the diagnosis was flawed and that customer orientation was not the problem. They agreed to meet at the consultancy's office to discuss the matter further.

A few days before the meeting, the management of the company received a letter from the consultancy saying that for reasons of office refurbishment the venue had been changed to a temporary, rented downtown office. The company directors duly arrived five minutes before the scheduled time – 10 am. The receptionist said she had not been informed about their arrival. Their names were not on the visitors list but that could be solved by the secretary of the consultants concerned. They were told where to go and arrived at the waiting room, which turned out to be the secretary's workplace; she was smoking and making private telephone calls. They sat down and waited. On the table were two half-full ashtrays, some used paper coffee cups and a few newspapers. The secretary continued talking on the phone with a friend, discussing what they were planning to do the coming weekend.

When the call was finished she turned to her computer. One of the directors got up and told her why they had come. Again the same story, nothing in the schedule, even worse: the consultants were in a meeting with an important client. But OK, she would let them know.

It turned out that there was a misunderstanding; the consultants were going to conclude their meeting and they would be available in a few minutes. Would the gentlemen like some tea? Sorry, no coffee, because the coffee machine was out of order this morning. No, the gentlemen did not want any tea, thank you very much. After 15 minutes the situation had not changed. One of them spoke and told the secretary that if the meeting didn't get started within five minutes they would leave and that that would have dire consequences for the relationship between the company and the agency. "I'll ask again," she said indifferently as if it was all very unimportant. "The meeting must be taking a bit longer, but it should be finished soon. Mr. Vines asks if you could just wait a few minutes more please. Would you like tea? Oh yes, I remember, I'm sorry." They had spent more than half an hour now without coffee in a cold, uncomfortable and dirty waiting room opposite an uninterested secretary waiting for what was obviously a badly planned appointment. Their patience ended, but as they started getting ready to leave, the door opened and the consultants came in. "Good morning," one of them said. "We hope you will forgive us for not being able to explain it in any other way, but you have just seen a demonstration of what many clients experience when they visit your offices."

For those professionals that are unsure of their customer orientation level, we offer the following self-assessment checklist. The seven points follow more or less the work process time sequence (input, throughput and output):

1. For whom am I working at the moment? For myself or for a customer? If I am working for myself, why am I doing that? Are there others that benefit from this? Who assesses the result of what I am doing and who is paying for it?

2. If I am working for a client, is that a potential client or a client I know by name? If I am working for a potential client, how do I know if the client could possibly be interested in the result of my work? When and how am I going to confront the client with that result?

3. If I am working for a *real* client, am I doing what he asked me to do? Do I know what is expected of me? In other words, do we agree on the output specifications? Is the request really from the client or did I – partly – formulate it myself?

4. At knowledge-intensive organizations the rule is: *quality is doing what you promised.* Am I doing what I promised to do? Did I not promise too much? Can I substantially deliver what I promised,

and can I do that within the agreed time-frame and budget? In other words, am I expert enough to do the work?

5. Do I really know if clients are satisfied with my work? If not, why do I not know that? If so, how do I know? Do you sense it, do I deduct that from the clients' attitude or do we together evaluate how it went and what has been achieved?
6. If the client evaluates the quality of my work, can I make a distinction between his satisfaction with my expertise and his satisfaction with my approach?
7. Am I not doing more of the same? Am I perhaps a victim of pigeon-holing? Does a certain amount of routine encroach on my work because of the type of work that I accept? Do I do that to make life easy for myself, or to achieve a higher turnover (money), or because I want to specialize even more in those type of tasks, or because I find it difficult to learn new methods and techniques? Do I still enjoy challenges in my work and why is that?

Just a bit more on the statement made under item 4: quality is doing what you promised, no more and no less.

Quality improvement programs that cannot be summarized like that are insufficiently constructive, place the emphasis on the wrong spot (on the rules and not on the people), deny the fact that most people are sincere and rather do something right than wrong and always cost more than they deliver (because of the inherent large overheads).

Here as before: get rid of those impersonal systems (debureaucratize according to the 80/20 rule) and learn to trust the self-managing capability of professionals. An enabling condition for the success of that approach: the presence of a collective ambition.

Intuition

We promised to address the importance of intuition in making strategic choices. No soft talk but just a few educative and self-explanatory real-life examples.

From an interview with Dr. Morris Chang, founder and chairman of the board of Taiwan Semiconductor Manufacturing Company:

When it comes to making business decisions, do you follow certain strategic principles?

How do I make strategic decisions? Well, I generally try to consider all angles. There's a Chinese poem: Du shang gao lou, wang jin tian ya lu – *"Alone you climb to the high tower, and then you see all the roads to the end of the world." Basically, it means you have to take a very macro view; you have to anticipate all the paths that lie ahead.*

Before I make a decision, I try to do that. I try to climb up to the high tower and look at all the consequences.

Is that a matter of analysis or intuition?

I think it's both, but more intuition than analysis because usually there isn't much data that you can analyze.

(The view from the high tower; Accenture, *Outlook 2002/1*)

Wim van der Leegte, MD of a steel construction company with 4,000 employees and a turnover of over 700 million dollars about his approach:

"It really is quite simple to turn a poorly run company around. You count the number of support staff. Then you count the number of production staff. For each support staff member you must have at least five in production. If that is not the case, then the overheads are too high and support staff must be reduced. That is what we call the "one to five rule." Thanks to these kind of rules of thumb things went like clockwork and I got bored. But I need a bit of stress so I took over more companies. First small ones here in the area. Later larger ones and ones located farther away. We always take it easy, on average two or so companies per year. There is no big strategic plan in which direction we should move. That's all bullshit. Whatever crosses our path we take. That is our policy.

(*NRC Handelsblad*, 15 July 2003)

About Christopher Columbus:
– The plans he made never matched what he actually did later.
– When he was underway he did not know where to go.
– When he got there, he did not know what he had found.
– And all of that was enthusiastically financed by others.

Strategy is what we do here and now. We also have future plans and we can see certain patterns in what already has happened. But the simple question of, "Have we made something we can sell, or have we sold what we could make?" remains unanswered. "The market" is a fantasy. Our organizational strategies are deeply inwardly focused.

(Niklas Luhmann, 1984)

"The core of Buddhist spirituality revolves around the perception that the unenlightened human lacks the mental discipline to exercise his own force of imagination: overwhelmed by this force, human beings lose themselves in self-created, egocentric imaginations of reality. To lose oneself in that imagination is something Buddhists call 'avidyā,' loosely translated as ignorance.'"
(Han de Wit, 1998)

Finally

Strategy for knowledge-intensive organizations is increasingly about reflecting on what has been done rather than making plans of what to do. Then use those reflections to recognize patterns that can eventually be elevated into a strategy.

"The wise man manages his affairs without acting and that way nothing remains not done," said Lao Tse. Do not organize and you get organization.

The person who can handle uncertainty enjoys this game the most; he who wins gets on the podium, and he who loses has learned the most.

We all know of course those funny acronyms which are so popular in the world of management, where everything begins with the same letter and which is, because of this, raised to the status of a model: the 7S model, the 5P model, the 9Cs, the 12Ks, and so on and so on.

For those people who would not buy this book if there were not at least one such acronym in it, we hereby quote the 5Fs of Rosbeth Moss Kanter, from the time when she was chief editor of the *Harvard Business Review*:

The five Fs of the new competitive organization:

Focused	⇒ make choices; concentrate on core competencies and core activities
Fast	⇒ debureaucratize; give people breathing space and steering capacity
Flexible	⇒ be inward looking; look from the outside in and innovate
Friendly	⇒ be friendly to people, planet, and profit
Fun	⇒ "If it's no fun, nobody is going to do any of this"

In these two chapters, we mainly wrote about collective ambition (What values and motives bind us together?) and strategy (How are we going to realize our [higher] goals?). In addition, the strategy repertoire contains three other important terms that have not been addressed thus far:

1. Mission (Why are we doing what we do?),
2. Vision (Where do we want to be in a few years?) and
3. Goals (What exactly do we want to achieve this year?).

3 STRUCTURE

Stimulate borderless cooperation through loosely defined and multiform structures

Why are many Continental European companies – working in the "Rhineland-tradition," see the explanation in the Introduction – increasingly more or just as successful in many areas than their American and British counterparts? The short answer is: it is the result of longer-term strategies involving cross cooperation. The "Rhinelanders" are more outward-looking, constantly on the lookout for opportunities. They do not shun cooperation with other manufacturers who are good at things that they themselves would never be good at, and this cooperation results in combining strengths. Rhineland coffee companies in continental Europe do not waste their time making individually competitive coffee machines; instead they get together with electronics companies that can. The same is true for Dutch beer brewers and Germany's Braun electronics; they got together to make a home draught beer system. And what about electric shavers using integrated sachets of facial cream to provide a smoother shave – a technology that is the result of cooperation between Nivea Cosmetics and Philips Electronics. While all this has been taking place, US coffee makers and brewers have been adding more and more flavors to their coffee and beer, but are in the process destroying the real taste of coffee and beer. But this latter strategy is easier and focuses on short-term success; but the companies are losing out in the long run to the detriment of the customer. They have become paranoid about losing their competitive edge. Losing that is something the shareholders most definitely do not want to hear at the next AGM four months from now.

Rhineland companies do not fire people when things are turning sour. They promote a stable atmosphere for people to feel comfortable in the longer term. Governments provide legislation that promotes job and income security because, in the end, companies and governments know that it will pay off. A few real-life examples:

"All Nokia phones out!"

Recently, Nokia decided to transfer one of their large manufacturing plants from Bochum, Germany, to Bulgaria because labor costs there are (still) very low. There was a big outcry in Germany about this. Angela Merkel, the German chancellor, was so disappointed about this unilateral decision that she asked all members of parliament to stop using Nokia phones, which they promptly did. At the time of writing, the minister-presidents of the individual German states were about to do the same thing. Can you see the US president doing the same thing with Motorola if they were to transfer one of their plants to Mexico?

"Please leave the boss out of it"

A meeting at a small US oil company was discussing the forward testing program on a well that they had just drilled. A lot of money had already gone into drilling and testing this well and a final effort was going to be made to get the well "to come in." In other words, it was a very important meeting. The company CEO was not at this meeting. After a while, everyone at the meeting agreed on a program strategy and the CEO was called in to give it the final approval for go ahead. After being told what the plan was, he totally opposed it and wanted something else. He was not convinced that the plan was right and wanted a second opinion from outside experts. I asked John, who had organized the meeting, if it would not have been better if the CEO had been at the meeting from the start. That way he would have been part of the solution and most likely he would not have been so obstructive. "No way," John said, "I never get him into these meetings because from the beginning he will disrupt proceedings and dominate it. The meeting will take far too long and we end up even more confused with more questions than answers. He always has his own agenda. It's either stop or go or go right or go left, but we never fully know the reasons. Today it wasn't go either right or left, but stop." This is so typical of what happens when the company is the CEO – with the shareholders breathing down his neck – and not the accumulation of workers. In such a setting, weak CEOs take decisions driven by shareholders, which are erratic and short term and hence are understood by no one in the company. There is only one shared vision everyone un-

derstands and that is satisfying the stakeholders. It has an enormous de-motivating effect on the professionals which perhaps explains why there is such high staff turnover at this type of **"My-way-or-the-highway"** *companies so typical of the Anglo-American model.*

Outward-looking companies that are run like this show symptoms of ADHD behavior (Attention Deficit Hyperactivity Disorder). *It is the best known and most common disorder among children. ADHD is char-acterized by a combination of the following symptoms: hyperactivity, impulsiveness and lack of concentration.*
Hyperactivity: always busy, lots of talking, always running around, al-ways out of breath.
Impulsiveness: always disruptive, jumping the gun, ignoring other opin-ions, shooting from the hip.
Lack of concentration: not listening, easily distracted, can't get organ-ized, can't finish the job, and avoids issues that need profound reflection. Sound familiar?

Or maybe not:

"Instead of ego or a narrow fix-it focus a well rounded leader eager to delegate?"
Will the Anglo-American model finally turn around to become more Rhineland like? Let's hope so. According to Nelson D Schwartz in an ar-ticle in the New York Times *(Nov 12, 2007), the time has come for the CEO to be a team player. After the downfall of the "empire builders," not to mention their profiles in the 1990s, with CEOs like Weill, Levin, Welch Jr. and Eisner, came the "fix-it men" with lower profiles to repair the mistakes of their predecessors. Now these boys are falling like ripe ap-ples and the time seems ripe for a different kind of CEO who can deal with environmental demands. Enter the "team builder." Enter the Rhineland model? Who knows, but it seems logical. According to Ben-nis, CEOs need an "ability to make people feel like they're working to-gether." They need "to make sure that the top one hundred people know that they are in this together." One hundred in companies with thou-sands of employees does not sound like a lot in the Rhineland model, but it could be a start in getting everyone involved and elevated towards a collective ambition for a workplace where people matter more.*

How to turn things around

For a flying start: what follows below are the rock-bottom demands that have to be made on the organizational structure of a knowledge-intensive organization. If your organization does not meet these demands, stop reading now and start working on them. (Although you have to read it first to know what to work on ...)

The structure of a knowledge-intensive organization:
- Facilitates the execution of the strategy ("Structure follows strategy")
- Offers a frame of reference for defining tasks, authorization and responsibilities, (task = answer to the question *what* needs to be done; responsibility = answer to the question of *who* has to do that; authority = answer to the question of *how* those responsibilities can be realized, which material and immaterial means are available)
- Gives the path of the horizontal and vertical lines of communication ·
- Shows who is responsible for the coordination of the various tasks and work areas
- Outlines the necessary structures of consultation
- Is flat, but does not lead to large spans of control (not more than approximately 30 professionals who report directly to the same superior)
- Can be unequivocally translated into a budgetary system with cost allocation
- Promotes collaboration and discourages territorial instinct and competency infighting
- Is flexible

The well-known and also profound structure question:
"Where do I fit in?"

At the end of the day, John wanders into Dave's office, a Marlboro filter casually between his fingers. The small and pale looking vice president of Social Strategy leans over a flip chart drawing a complicated diagram with arrows, and boxes and dotted lines. He starts when he sees John.

"I am preparing an outline for a modified organizational chart for top management."

"So," said John, "you don't sit still do you?" He studied the diagram briefly.
"Reserved yourself a cushy spot?"
"Oh, I am not that far yet, this is just an organizational concept, more as an example to clarify the structure."
(Vermeulen Windsant)

Managers always want to change the structure, driven by one or more of the following motives:

1. Because they want to show some achievements.

2. Because they have nothing else to do because the professionals are already intrinsically motivated.
   Driven by their trade and the collective ambition, the professionals are self-managing and they would much rather do something right than wrong, so you have nothing to worry about. Managers who, due to a lack of specialized knowledge, cannot really get excited about what is going on in the workplace and – as a result of the advancing Anglo-American business model, we have more and more of those – are getting bored. They find that "management by wandering around"[*] is useless, while it is actually the ideal management style for a knowledge-intensive organization. They long for macho dynamics, want to score and therefore often choose to tackle the structure because that is the easiest thing to change and always causes most waves.

3. Because changing the organizational structure is not that difficult and it is always great to communicate about it with other managers.
   Tasks, authorities, and responsibilities can be digitally re-distributed if you want to implement, say, business units, integral management or result-responsible units. Sections can easily be split up, merged, created, eliminated, or placed somewhere else and you can make attractive graphs of before and after: "When I started here, the situation was like this; now, after three months, the

[*]   See Chapter 6.

organization is like this." We all know such shows. And you can use it to score with higher management who are generally even more enthusiastic about structural changes, because the higher up in the hierarchy, the greater the focus on structure. "Look, here you can still see that there was a management layer between the product group managers and the unit leaders and now, after the flattening operation, that has disappeared, has been taken out. You can also see very clearly here the new product-oriented front-stage organization that is depicted at the top of the inverted pyramid, with its face towards the customer. Underneath there is a discipline-oriented backstage supporting the front office. If you listen carefully you can hear them shout: more, more!"

The upside of it is that for a sleepy and self-indulgent organization changing the structure is potentially a good way of livening things up a bit.

In most cases, however, it makes no difference; it merely costs a lot of time, many rounds of meetings, and it stimulates territorial instinct and competency infighting. It can cause unpleasant job-hopping and the result of all that fuss can be a marginal improvement or a marginal deterioration. Yet managers can't get enough of it. They continue with it enthusiastically as if it were *"l'art pour l'art."* But changing structures is no art. "Everyone can make nice graphs."

"What in hell does he do all this for?"

An organization with over 1,000 employees has just appointed a new Managing Director, a young man who, with little more than an MBA under his belt, is making a big step forward in his career. Possibly too big because, just after he was introduced to his immediate colleagues, he set out to change all sorts of things, even though the company was doing fine. Such ambition is often a sign of insecurity that is hiding behind a lot of energetic action. Instead of first trying to get a picture by observing and inquiring in the traditional first 100 days, the new top dog thought he already knew exactly what the situation was after just a week and a half. From then on, activity A had to be outsourced, the problem in department B had to be solved by turning it into a support unit reporting directly to him, units C and D had to be merged and brought under one manager, plenary meeting E was abolished due to its redundancy, the service concerned with F could be shrunk by 30% and he wanted to sign off personally on all reports about subject G.

The consequences were dramatic. First there was confusion, then resistance and obstruction, followed by attempts to understand these structural interventions and when that was unsuccessful, people simply continued as if nothing had happened. They did their work and totally ignored the new manager as if he didn't even exist. The professionals indicated that they no longer wanted to be kept from doing their important work by incomprehensible, egoistic solo actions from this newcomer. They nodded understandably when he mentioned further changes, said politely that they thought it would not improve things and went on with their usual work. As a consequence, the new boss became totally isolated and he found it increasingly difficult to obtain his management information on time.

In the end, the Board asked him to leave the building with a precious metal handshake. The formal explanation was that he did not have a vision or at least had been unable to get it across.

In reality what had happened was that he made changes for the sake of change, but had no idea which direction he wanted to take with the organization.

Alfred Chandler, Professor at MIT and Harvard, wrote way back in 1962: "Structure follows strategy." But if you don't know where to go, any structure will do.

4. Because structure is still the favorite variable for managers. They cannot leave it alone!

That is because they think that organizing is the same as structuring. If the tasks, authorities, and responsibilities have been distributed and the lines of reporting are fixed, then the rest will come by itself. Or so they think. Not so! The professionals swallow the macho-managerial language. They know these kinds of stories, have heard them so often before. They know that in the end the informal structure, the collaboration culture, becomes stronger after each of these formal structural changes.

At knowledge-intensive organizations, most power is concentrated with the professionals in the primary process. Hence, if you really want to change the structure, you always have to make sure that the new structure is in harmony with the informal cooperation culture. Managers who do not see this, will end up in a self-created virtual reality that has little or nothing to do with the way professionals actually function.

The manager spends so much time thinking about and discussing the new structure with so many outsiders that he has little energy left to formulate the process change. That is why related change processes are often messy spectacles, makeshift repairs, patchwork, surrealistic scenes. The manager does his thing no matter what; he improvises as if he is a surrealistic painter. Motives for change are forced down people's throats and rationality is totally absent. In the end, nobody has a clue as to what he is on about. Consequently, this leads to lots of unproductive discussions, especially amongst junior professionals who have not learned yet how to continue unperturbed with their work in spite of all the fuss.

White smoke is not enough; professionals want to understand the process!

It has become common: administrators and managers take all the time in the world to prepare for a merger or a strategic alliance. For months they deliberate and negotiate, weigh and wait, dine and hold conference calls. Then finally the day has arrived when little kingdoms are handed out to every manager's satisfaction and the intention to merge is announced to "the organization." Everybody gathers in the entry hall or the company's restaurant for the important announcement by the top dog. In modern organizations it is done even more efficiently and remotely with an e-mail or a video message to all staff. Then the top is amazed at the cool reception the announcement gets. The management has taken months to become accustomed to and to accept the new situation; it now has to be digested by the staff in a considerably shorter time, preferably that very same day.

A typical illustration of this pattern can be read in a farewell interview with the dean of a university: "Three years ago a merger with another university was almost a done deal at the administrative level. The boards and even the Minister of Education had followed the process with interest and appeared positive. The champagne was ready. Then when the plan leaked (!) there appeared to be a lot of resistance from scientists and other staff members of both universities. I thought I would be telling them good news, but it was impossible to sail against this current."

Another illustration – but on a much larger scale – were the referenda that were held about the European constitution; it failed to get the support of the majority of the people in France and the Netherlands, and more recently the Irish. The governments of these countries that put the European constitution out to a referendum had failed to involve the people from the outset. But the opposition politicians who were against it did try to involve the public. This proved easy with slogans such as "no more bureaucrats" and "France for the French." When the polls started showing a possible defeat, cabinet ministers and politicians tried to persuade the voters but by then the harm was done. They were too late. The public felt left out and the whole thing nosedived, no matter how beneficial it was for the people.

Administrators toast the successful result while the people in the workplace know nothing about it. Unless the advantages are crystal clear, such an approach is doomed to failure.

Managers do not want to make an internal statement until everything is done and dusted. Otherwise, they think, they do not have a "good story." But research shows that if people are involved in an organizational change from an early stage, they are much more inclined to accept such a change, and that acceptance is even stronger when it concerns professionals. It pays to say at a certain point that you do not know something. "This and this has been arranged, we are negotiating about such and such, and we do not yet know how we are going to tackle issue X. That is mainly because ..." Such an approach is much more productive than waiting until all differences are straightened out and hoping that nothing will leak.

The manager or administrator who only informs "the organization" after everything has been resolved, is too late and cannot count on much support. Professionals who have never learned to deal with uncertainties cannot do anything other than be for or against it.

So what is the solution? I (MW) have published a lot on knowledge management. That includes essays about the functional, the operational and the matrix structure. Also on modern forms such as the self-steering team or cell structure, the web structure, the hypertext structure and fuzzy structuring.

For the purpose of this book, however, it is sufficient to mention a set of five general ground rules for setting up a structure for a knowledge-intensive organization, stimulating creativity with the remark that there are many structures that potentially meet the terms of those five rules.

The fuzzy structure of a management consultancy

The design of the fuzzy structure is based on the following:
– we downplay the importance of the formal structure
– along the way, through self-organization, we find out, bottom-up, which is the most common structure in use
– we allow many groups, many growth kernels; there is no minimum or maximum size per group

- group composition is based on personal preferences (trade, product, market, learning environment, personal affinity, etc.)
- senior staff and partners are allowed to be a member of a maximum of three groups; juniors and associates may be a member of only one group
- the group elects a leader from its midst, for a period of three years
- we decentralize and delegate as much as possible in order to effectuate the advantages of a flat organization (short lines, speed and flexibility)

The implementation of the agency's fuzzy structure had four steps:

Step 1
- Each manager/advisor chooses the colleagues she or he wants to form a team with, based on valid and strong reasons
- Commitment to the team is, in principle, for three years; an intermediate transfer to another team needs the approval of the members of the receiving team (application obligation)
- Execution: meeting at a conference center with a large plenary room with as many round tables as there are teams
- Professionals who want to be in the same team, sit at the same table. Intensive bilateral en multilateral communication preceding meetings are probable and make sense. Procedures for try-out rounds, interesting team compositions, criteria for team choice and the like are brought in for support

Step 2
- The team adopts a name (Marketing Team Industry, Product Team Communication Management, Subject Team Telemetries, the Warhol Team, the Phoenix Team, Team 14, etc.).
- Each team mutually agrees the team leader's tasks, powers and responsibilities

Step 3
- Each team elects a leader
- The commitment of the leader is in principle three years; re-election is possible

Step 4
Every three years: repeat steps 1, 2 and 3 for various reasons: break out of the rut and routine, avoid pigeon-holing, learn from others, adapt to changed market circumstances, liven things up

Design Rule 1: Formalize the structure only on main principles
This is done in order to facilitate a synergy searching collaborative culture, which is possible only if higher management considers the informal and formal structure of equal importance. The professionals already agree on this but management may still have a problem. Management needs to appreciate the collaborative structure more than the organizational structure; they must realize that the structure that has grown informally has become the collaborative culture. A consequence of this rule is that to sin against the formal structure, like treading into others' territories, or to seize adjacent powers, is not (or hardly) seen as unacceptable as long as it is in the interest of the organization and the customer.

It must be obvious that a loosely formalized structure promotes development, maintenance and an innovative combining and applying of (core) competencies. It also makes *parallel processing* and *concurrent engineering* easier.

This first rule also makes sure that changing the formal structure (if so required) can easily be done. Changes can even be made on a daily basis, as long as they are aimed at adapting the formal structure to the dynamics of the collaborative culture created by the professionals. That is, do not create too wide a gap between formal and informal structures; try to keep up with the autonomous developments in the informal structure with formal structural changes.

Design Rule 2: Aim to lay the accountability for the result at the lowest possible level, so preferably with the professionals themselves and opt for integral management if the level of ambition is not that high
At a knowledge-intensive organization, allow the department or team commitment to be the sum of personal commitments (see also Chapter 4). So no pass-the-buck models with integrated managers and (business) unit leaders who are accountable for the results of their subordinates. This is because the professionals hold most of the knowledge to determine which methods or techniques, products or services are needed to meet the customers' wishes.

Governmental, health care, and educational organizations, even the judiciary, are still trying to introduce integrated management.

Policy makers, surgeons, professors, and judges are asked to manage everything: understand budgets and financial procedures, be familiar with recruitment, selection, staff reporting and reward bonuses, manage the organization, etc. What a waste of expensive education; what a shame that their expertise is being diluted by all these non-core activities; how sad that they have less time to apply their experience and skills.

Experience has taught us that only if an organization fosters a modest activity-related ambition can the advantages of integrated management outweigh the disadvantages. This means a *middle-of-the-road* ambition with a *me too* strategy with regard to products and services and with much more attention to efficiency than to innovation. In this environment, with an almost total lack of professional pride, even someone with an MBA degree can keep the shop running.

There is a direct correlation between strategic ambition and integrated management: from content-expert foreman (80% hands-on 20% management) at the highest ambition level, via integrated manager (40-60% hands-on; 60-40% management), to MBA/professional fixer (<20% hands-on; >80% management) with a very low level of expert ambition. However, when the knowledge-intensive organization is guided by financial and profit ambitions, then the correlation behaves the other way around: in particular the MBA man knows best how to optimize such an organization into a money-making machine.

Integral management can also be defended when the organization can be qualified as a holding of operating companies that provide products and services that have little in common and hardly encounter each other in the markets which they serve.

When a hands-on foreman identifies for himself a need for integrated management, then one must be careful. Such a wish can be an indication of diminishing professional expertise. When expertise is lacking, the fixer automatically appears.

FUNCTIONAL STRUCTURE:
The profession is key

MANAGEMENT

Compensating task for management:
Program management

E.g.: | Physics | Chemistry | Biotechnology | ITC | Mechatronics |

Secondary question: where is the operational leader who says WHAT to do?

OPERATIONAL STRUCTURE:
The end product is key

MANAGEMENT

Compensating task for management:
Provide the necessary professional expertise

E.g.: | Lasers | Optical systems | Digital memories | Magnetic media | Electro motors |

Secondary question: where is the functional leader who says HOW to do it?

MATRIX STRUCTURE: the interaction
between the professional and the program is key   MANAGEMENT

Compensating task for management:
Keep the matrix in balance

Program or project groups

Capability or trade groups

project managers
(knowledge application)

functional/department managers
(knowledge development)

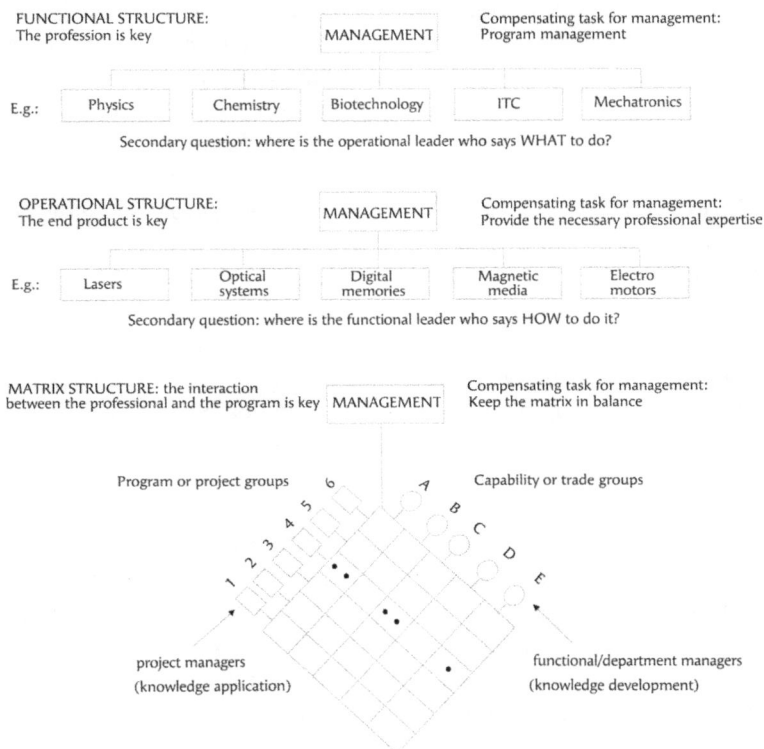

Design Rule 3: Go for a functional divide; go by discipline

Experts in one discipline should be grouped together, so that they can easily learn from each other and as such create a practice of socially conditioned (not top-down) peer review. Of course, there is the danger of creating a monomaniacal specialist culture that sinks ever deeper into an expert pit. It may also be difficult to allocate responsibility for the end result. The coordination between disciplines can take much time and effort. Yet these disadvantages do not outweigh the advantages; but all structures have the disadvantage that the arrangement that is not chosen lacks those advantages. The advantages of the functional structure are: the potential to grow into a center of excellence mainly because people can continuously learn from each other (= deep learning vs. broad learning), greater efficiency of the contribution required (anyone outside the discipline group can ask for super specialized input from the professional who is best placed to answer that particular question) and, if applicable, widespread use of precious production resources. This design rule has proven to be very effective, especially in beta and technology-driven knowledge-intensive organizations. There are many examples in that industry of organizations with a reputation as a center of excellence which share, as a second common characteristic, a functional structure.

Design Rule 4: Go for geographical concentration and a flat organizational structure

The knowledge-intensive organization must be physically concentrated at one location. Even then there are still lots of dos and don'ts for further synergetic interaction between the professionals. On the basis of research in R&D organizations, Tom Allen has shown that a staircase between two floors and even a swing door in a corridor has a negative influence on the frequency of the technical communication between workers and hence on the result. In addition to geographic concentration, it appears that flattening the organizational structure has a positive effect on professionals' job satisfaction, the synergy of their contributions and finding the – so important for innovation – "Neue Kombinationen" (new combinations).

Flattening

Each year, many managers in equally many parts of the world basically find themselves directing Bach's St. Matthew Passion. Each of these directors directly manages more than 100 employees without intervening layers. Most organizations would rate such a large span of control excessive and even irresponsible. Orchestras do not have a problem with that because the objective is crystal clear. Everyone knows what is expected of them. That clear objective makes sure that the amount of emails, meetings, and reports are kept to a minimum. "Yes but without extra layers the director needs to conduct over 100 staff reports. That can't be done," is the criticism. With the St. Matthew Passion that is not an issue because there is no need for such rituals. If an employee plays or sings very beautifully, the other musicians show their appreciation by stamping their feet on the floor. If some-one is not that good, the director consults with him or her and some section colleagues on how best to rectify the situation.

What really counts is the ability of the director to inspire. Inspiration leads to involvement and to extreme commitment by the employees. Each layer between the inspiring leader and the professionals in the workplace increases the interference in communication and dampens the motivation.

We knew all this some ten years ago. Organizational flattening – de-layer-ing – was common in those days. The management pyramids collapsed like melting chocolate and broadened at the base where self-steering teams took charge. Now the management layers are again on the increase. Stimu-lated by all-pervasive IT, the vertical control increases anew and one super structure after the other appears. The team is managed by the department, the department by the product-market group, the product-market group by the business line, which in turn is managed by the business unit, which is directed by the division, which is governed by HQ, as part of the Holding, etc. In the public sector it is sometimes even worse; the group belongs in a department, the department is part of the main department, the main de-partment belongs to the service, the service is part of the directorate, the di-rectorate participates in the program group, the program group is part of the division, the division has to pay attention to what the inter-divisional coordination group says and so on and so on.

All those layers have their own management, supervisors, and support staff and hence cost a lot of money. That they cost lots of time makes it even worse for the shop floor. They are prevented from doing their work in a big way, thanks to meetings, coordination consultations, evaluation meetings, program discussions, budget rounds and so on. In short, man-agement layers add time and money with no added value.

An old Jewish proverb says that if you want to irritate the competition wish them lots of personnel. In our present time, you would say: "I wish you many management layers." Apparently, we all have a tremendous dislike for each other since that wish is being fulfilled on a grand scale.

Design Rule 5: Install a double or triple career development ladder (DDL)

Shell's career development system

Although Shell is an Anglo-Dutch company it is very much what you would call an Anglo-American type company. When I (CH) started out at Shell as a young engineer in the 1970s, there was a performance evaluation system that dominated the corporate culture. In fact, to this day Shell still uses this system, albeit in a somewhat different form. The aim, however, is still the same: to manage and monitor someone's career progress. But more importantly for young engineers and geologists, it is used to determine early on who has management potential and who does not. Bosses were required to write "staff reports" on the performance of their subordinates every year. The results of these reports were extremely important to the career of the individual. A report consisted of two parts: part one would deal with the actual performance and part two would deal with the impression the boss had of the employee as a person. Did he have a high level of imagination, was he analytical, did he have a "sense of reality," did he radiate marked leadership, and did he have "helicopter view." All these traits would add up to what was called the "Ultimate Potential" i.e. the job level that one would achieve at the height of one's career given unlimited job opportunities. The second part was supposed to have no real relationship with the outcome of part one; in fact you could theoretically be a real "slacker" in part one but get a high potential in part two. Great plan! But ... obviously every ambitious engineer wanted to score high on the UP but in order to do that you had to be seen to be a manager and certainly not a "nerd." Experts at Shell never get higher up in the Shell hierarchy (read salary group) than a middle manager would. So no one who was ambitious would ever tell his boss that management was not really his "thing." The result of this should be obvious to everyone. The emphasis was on showing how good one was in social and communicative skills rather than doing a good job in the chosen discipline. Under such a system every ambitious young academic wanted to be a manager! That is where you could get high salaries and recognition. The result: middle and higher managers that are not particularly happy in their leading role but could have been brilliant and happy specialists. Things are, however, changing slowly. Recently, Shell "invented" what they call senior specialists, six in total – one per discipline – who were given a status equal to that of a top-level manager. What a prospect for a young ambitious person who prefers engineering to management!

Fortunately, career possibilities other than line management – so called DDL – are becoming more popular. The reason for this, illustrated in the example above, is the growing opinion that good managers are often not good professionals and vice versa. "Each his own trade," or "You can't be good at everything," is what people say, or when promoting a professional to manager: "We have lost a good professional and got a bad manager instead." The best professional wants to be rewarded appropriately because he or she is the best professional. If the organization only provides the opportunity to make him or her a manager, then that is – except maybe in a materialistic sense – not seen by the professional as a reward because – as a result of this move – he will do less of what he is so good at: his profession.

In a technology-intensive R&D lab where I (MW) worked, that was clearly recognized. One day I asked: "How do you select your new group leaders?" One of the board members answered: "We select someone from the group itself. Not the best professional, of course, that would be a waste. We ask someone who is reasonably good in his profession, but who has above average communicative skills. He must also be prepared to buy a tie and attend receptions."

In order to offer well-performing professionals an inspiring perspective and to contradict the concept of "If I want to get ahead I have to become a manager," somebody came up with the *dual ladder*. A career structure with two parallel tracks, one for the manager and one for the professional in which the career potential for both would be virtually equal.

The knowledge worker on the professional ladder should therefore also be entitled to stock options, a lease car with metallic paint, a parking space near the entrance, a leather chair with a high back, a large wooden desk, high-tech IT stuff, a small fridge in their room with a nice view, and so on.

The management ladder is for those who like the management buzz and like to play boss (I recently visited such a manager for an interview. When I entered his office, he said with a commanding voice: "We have scheduled one hour in my diary; we'll make do with 45 minutes, because I have 700 people here hanging round my neck." I smiled because I could literally see that. The way he said it, gave me the impression that his ultimate goal would be to have twice as many hanging around his neck). In practice, however, when you're on the management ladder there is only attention for time and money, with plan-to-do action and **operational excellence**. Process management of collective ambition development, which is also part of that line, is generally under-addressed. *Short-time business drives out long-term business* and that is why more time is spent on the nitty-gritty than on thinking about strategy for the company; something that in many cases only seems to be possible during specially planned "away days."

On the professional line it is entirely different. There you see the responsibility for **innovation**, for technological/product/service leadership. HR and finance are merely a nuisance. The dual ladder professional has no one hanging around his neck. He does not need to dilute his exclusive expertise in his discipline with branch-alien activities. He does, however, participate in all sorts of internal and external knowledge networks and he has a small pot of money with which he can form ad hoc groups to work on certain breakthrough projects that do not fit into the standard programs (radical and out of-the-box innovations). The dual ladder professional uses that money to compensate the leaders of the groups from which he occasionally borrows professionals to work under his leadership on such innovation projects.

He personally asks these people to work on his project and usually they find it an honor to be asked, because it means your professional expertise is recognized by a top professional. Also they find it captivating and educational to work for such a master in the discipline.

Because the question: "Stay a professional or become a manager?" is only relevant after a number of years in the trade, the DLL has taken on the shape of a Y.

Then some enlightened managers (who still had Chapter 2 fresh in their memories) thought: "Of the three determining factors for the generic strategy of the knowledge-intensive organization, we have now, with the dual ladder, translated two of the lines into a structure: operational excellence on the management line and innovation on the professional line. Why not give the last one – customer intimacy or **customer orientation** – a supporting structure?" This equally logical as well as rational insight has resulted in the *triple ladder* of development; by adding a commercial or account management line, the DLL evolves from a Y into a ψ. Proctor and Gamble are a good example of this. There, younger engineers become product managers early in their career and promote a particular product like Gillette razors or a detergent. This middle career line is for people that like to play in the street. If you want to excel in your profession throughout your professional life, you progress up the professional ladder. If, after a number of years, you find it increasingly difficult to stay in your profession and you decide you would really like to be a boss of something, you can go on the management ladder. If you can do neither but quite like the club around you and if you have good social and communicative skills, well then you can follow the commercial line.

There is an old story about a major manufacturer who hired an efficiency expert to evaluate his company. After many weeks, the expert reported to the president of the company that everyone seemed to work with maximum efficiency, with the exception of one man, a Mr. Drummond.

"I've passed Mr. Drummond's office every day for nearly a month," said the efficiency expert, "and every time, without exception, Mr. Drummond was sitting with his feet up on his desk, his hands behind his head, and with his eyes closed. Well, I checked Mr. Drummond's salary, and do you realize that you pay him more than you pay most of your vice presidents? Really, I advise you to get rid of him!" The president of the company considered the advice for a moment, made a phone call and, when he hung up, replied to the efficiency expert as follows. "Let me tell you about Mr. Drummond. One day, about five years ago, Mr. Drummond was sitting with his feet up on his desk, his hands behind his head, and with his eyes closed, and then this same Mr. Drummond invented a process that saves this company ten million dollars a year. Mr. Drummond may sit, lie, stand on his head, or sleep for all I care, if that's how he gets his ideas!" (Root-Bernstein, 1989)

The greatest tension in the DDL structure lies between the commercial line and the professional line. The top professionals who – particularly in beta organizations – still think that technological quality sells itself, do not understand why their colleagues on the commercial ladder make so much money when they are on the golf course half the time, start work every day at ten or half past ten because they have been out dining the evening before.

"I also dined out yesterday evening, but I was here this morning on time like always while all they seem able to do is hand out and receive visiting cards! They then give those cards to us with a vague story that we should contact these people to help them solve their problems, but 9 out of 10 of these problems have already been solved. If they had bothered to read the literature they would have known that. Idiots!" The other day I asked one of these slick individuals if he knew Ohm's Law. He answered: "No, but bring him along, the more the merrier." The point is that knowledge workers on the professional line do not always realize that there is only one place where the cash register rings and that is in the market. If there is a demand it makes sense to sell sound solutions more than just once. The financial and economical sensitivity of professionals (especially technical professionals) is simply too low.

The triple career development ladder (TDL)

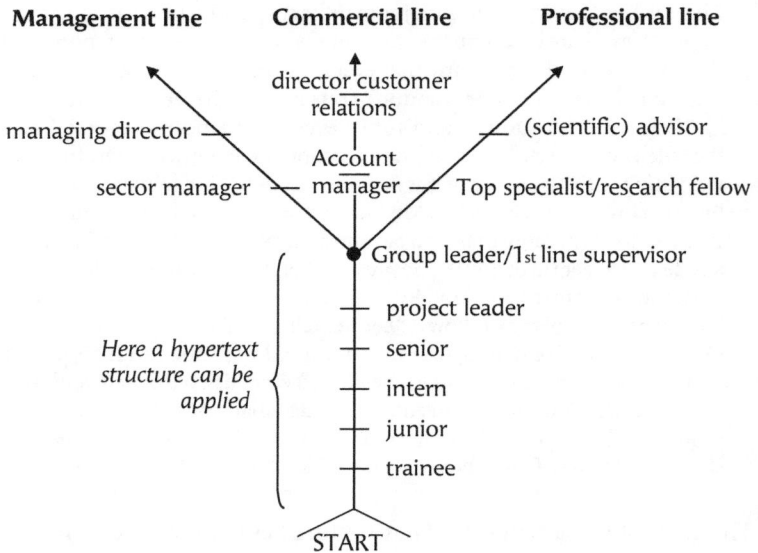

Management line	Commercial line	Professional line

director customer
relations

managing director → Account ← (scientific) advisor
manager

sector manager → manager ← Top specialist/research fellow

Group leader/1st line supervisor

Here a hypertext structure can be applied {
— project leader
— senior
— intern
— junior
— trainee

START

Formally implementing a DDL is the easy part. To subsequently use the three lines in the right way generally proves to be considerably more difficult. To make the DDL work for the professional line, a number of focus points are relevant:

- The number of functionaries on the professional line should never be less than about half of the functionaries on the management line (and may at most be equal). If admittance to the professional line is a relatively rare affair, an unbalanced structure will emerge.
- HR problems must never be solved with the help of the professional line. In organizations with a DDL, the professional line could be misused by HR. For example, for a professional with high seniority, who has made his mark in the past but is now at the end of his career and does not really know how to manage and doesn't even know whether he wants to manage. Even managers who do not function any longer at the required level, are sometimes transferred to the professional line to "cool off" in a fake "Special Assignment" from the Board, the result of which the Board has no interest in whatsoever. That way the professional line is totally

marginalized, and loses its credibility and attractiveness as a viable option for the best professionals.

- "Police the quality. A dual ladder is only as good as it is perceived to be. Consequently, make certain that only first class people get on it and those who are on it continue to do first class work. Should they cease performing, you must have some mechanism of moving them off in order not to tarnish its image. Nothing will destroy the dual ladder faster."
(Allen Heininger, *VP Research and Development*, Monsanto Co., in: Wolff, 1979).

- To follow on from the previous issue it is necessary to formalize carefully the admission to the professional ladder. EIRMA report number 40 on *Personal Management in R&D* (1990) presents a proper procedure. Although this procedure is tailored to R&D organizations, it seems obvious to use it in other professional organizations. "The system for promotion is very severe. It consists of an assessment of the scientific value of the nominated candidate established by a Committee of Wise Men on the basis of a list of criteria. These criteria are linked to the performance, the expertise, the role and relations of the candidate. There is a system of weighted marking (according to the importance of the criteria considered). A certain total must be attained for each level. Candidates are nominated by their managers and prepare their own file (publications, results, patents, reports). After the file has been examined by the Committee of Wise Men, the candidates are informed of the conclusion and receive feedback. Nobody may be nominated in two consecutive years." Employees on the professional line need a budget that they can use at their own discretion to finance innovation projects. Such a budget must be more than sufficient to pay the internal tariffs of a team of professionals, and to invest in the necessary investments in equipment, travel, external consultants, etc.

- Employees on the professional line must be exempt from the administration of personnel, finances, infrastructure and the like, with the exception of the responsibility for spending the program budget allocated to the DDL professional. In addition, it would make sense to get involved as an informer and/or co-assessor in performance assessments of those professionals who have worked

under the leadership of the DDL professional in the execution of innovation projects defined by him.
- It must be attractive to be on the professional ladder. That can be achieved by, say, creating several promotional steps.
- It is extremely important for the effectiveness of the DDL to institutionalize an explicit, systematic and periodic confrontation of the DDL professionals with the end users (customers) of the products and services that the organization provides. Only by creating such a connection in the product chain can DDL professionals be prevented from inventing in perfect isolation, wonderful things that nobody wants.

One might add that it would be good if professionals made a habit of putting a clause in their contract that stipulates that the number of potential promotional steps is unlimited so that the top can be reached by everybody on the dual ladder and that the potential number of demotion steps is no more than one. Such a clause would imply that *the sky is the limit* ("See you on the Board") but also that the professional can be asked once in his career to return to his previous or comparable position, while retaining the salary attached to the higher position. The advantages of such a provision are obvious. There is less chance of stress and burn out. A position that demands more knowledge than the worker possesses has a negative effect on the on the employee's well-being. With a provision such as the one proposed above, such negative influence is never long term. Furthermore, such a provision has the advantage that is satisfies "vertical" learning needs more quickly. In promotion decisions it will not be necessary to observe the highest level of certainty and in that respect one can take more risks. And finally, the chance – albeit with some delay – that the right person will end up in the right job increases considerably, avoiding the occurrence of the Peter Principle: "In a hierarchy every employee tends to rise to his level of incompetence. For every employee who rises above his level of competence, there are several whose full talents are not utilized."[*]

All this does not imply that one is obliged to apply the "1x-demotion rule;" it should only be applied when it cannot be avoided.

[*] Badawy, 1982

DDL and hypertext structure fit together well

The expression "hypertext structure" has been around for some time. It originates from the breakthrough work performed by Nonaka and Takeuchi in 1995: The Knowledge Creating Company. "Like an actual hypertext document, a hypertext organization is made up of interconnected layers or contexts." Generally, one can speak of a hypertext structure in an organization if the entire primary process has, with the help of at least two independent classification criteria, the same number of complete structures. That is, for instance, the case when a knowledge-intensive organization decides to organize its primary process both operationally (by product or service) and functionally (by discipline) and market oriented at one and the same time. That same process automatically has three structures: one operational, one functional, and one market oriented. These structures overlap each other whereby each structure covers the entire process. Each professional works in three structures at any one time. Should someone be interested in the organizational structure, the professional can rightfully ask: which of the three structures would you like to see? Because all three can apply at any moment. Hence the metaphoric link with hypertext is that if you click on a professional that you found in the functional chart you can see his position in the market oriented group. A professional in the primary process of such a hypertext organization could be a leader in the "magnetism" discipline group, while in the operational structure he could be a member of the product group "MRI Scanners" and "account manager region south" in the market oriented structure. This means that each arrangement has its own hierarchical structure, complete with meetings, staff reporting, rules and procedures and so on. What is nice is that the tangle of interrelations, the redundancy in the vertical coordination and the numerous trajectories that can be followed through the structure to reach your professional growth, ensure that any management other than on the basis of collective ambition, has little effect. After all, the authority-based model of planning & control that the hierarchical structure is based on, is in conflict with the interaction-filled way of working in the hypertext structure.

About the benefit of vagueness and redundancy in the ant world.

"Biologists are getting ever better insight into the way in which certain species integrate coincidence, uncertainty, and risk into the way they react to their surroundings. For example, the collective existence of ants is based on a recruiting mechanism. As soon as an ant has found a prey, he marks the route back to the nest with a scent. He gathers more ants from the nest, and these in turn intensify the scent track. Some are completely deterministic: the mustered ants go to the location without hesitation. Others are clearly less determined: sometimes some ants lose their way. Biologists assume that the fact that some recruitment messages become relatively inaccurate due to "interference" does not necessarily have to be disadvantageous. Such "interference" could present other opportunities. The ants that have gone astray could, for instance, find another prey, perhaps even a larger one. This hypothesis is based on correlations between recruitment mechanisms and surroundings: perfect recruitment seems to occur in areas where the prey is large but few, and the inaccurate recruitment occurs where the prey is generally smaller, but in greater numbers." (Stengers, 1986)

The professional has a full-time position in each parallel layer of the hypertext structure, while the total working time available remains constant. This means that whatever he does he will try to optimize the contributions he makes when fulfilling his two or three roles. You can compare this with a housewife who realizes that each task offers opportunities for her to optimize her roles as mother, spouse and citizen.

The great advantage of a hypertext structure is that it lets knowledge-intensive organizations develop evolutionary and organically without needing large, unnatural restructuring because alternative structures are permanently activated simultaneously, whereby it is possible, for instance, that in one period the functional structure is deemed more important and in next period the operational function is more dominant. The virtual lack of the need for structure interventions (managers have hardly any time for hobbies), means that perfect serenity reigns at an organization with a hypertext structure. All this only at the expense of a tiny reduction in short-term efficiency. That is mainly due to the redundancy and social slack required to switch between the various structure layers. In addition, the pleasure people have in their work and the continuity of the organization are both served well by a hypertext structure; compare this with the centuries-old, but in our view dramatically inefficient organizational structures of insects, birds and fish living in groups.

It must be clear to anyone by now that the hypertext structure is an ideal structure to implement dual and triple ladders. Those ladders enable professionals in the second phase of their career to convert to one of the divisions that is applied in the hypertext structure. There is a professional line for those who primarily want to restrict themselves to the functional structure and are permanent innovation enthusiasts. For a more dominant focus on the market-oriented structure there is the commercial ladder. And for those who like collective ambition development, inspiring people and operational excellence, there is the traditional management line.

How terrible is it to be a first-line manager?

A good first-line supervisor must rely on the respect and trust of his people because he is considered an expert. At the same time, he must possess the communicative skills to negotiate the necessary time and money with higher management. With a DDL there is a better chance of finding candidates in the organization that not only fulfill the requirements but are also prepared to spend a few years as a first-line supervisor. The reason for this is that there is a real perspective for them to make a choice out of several progressions on the basis of the experience gained: after a sabbatical leave to "catch up on knowledge" back to the old discipline, or progressing into the management line because you have discovered that you're good at it and strangely enough enjoy it, or you go up the commercial ladder because you like to play outside, or you are so good in your discipline that despite the time you needed to manage, you still qualify for a position on the professional ladder.

The collection of first-line managers (synonyms: group leaders, team leaders, unit leaders, discipline chairs, department chairs, chiefs, supervisors) form the backbone of every knowledge-intensive organization. If all top-level managers go off together to play golf for three months in Barbados, the organization will continue to function as normal. Should the first-line managers decide to go to Disneyland for three weeks, the organization would grind to a halt within a few days.

Such an observation sheds an interesting light on the discussion about top salaries. Word has it that the reward at the top of the pyramid has to remain the highest and should even be increased, because otherwise you cannot get good people. The higher the top salaries, the more you can offer the people on the lowest level. The thought behind this is that the work gets more difficult and the responsibility greater the higher you climb, and that the material reward has to keep up. In the industrial age that made sense, and it makes sense in today's public office but not in the present-day knowledge economy. Today, the most difficult job and the highest responsibility lies with the professionals in the workplace, the doctors, the judges, the teachers, the engineers, the police inspectors, the researchers. And the most difficult job in a knowledge organization is that of first-line manager of a group of professionals. That is the only level where the combination of professional substance and management knowledge is vital. If a group leader does not understand the profession he will not be taken seriously by his professionals and if he is not familiar with budgets, procedures and performance indicators he cannot look after the interests of his group. Nowhere else in a knowledge-intensive organization is uncertainty and the risk of stress and burnout so high as among first-line managers. Hence, they need to get the highest pay; more than the professionals who work every day in their discipline and more than managers above them for whom the profession plays only a marginal role.

It is extremely tough, and if the first-line supervisor is to stay healthy, it is better not to do this work longer than say four years and then to hand it over to someone else.

How high is high?

Lama Govinda said that each individual at some point has to make a choice between striving for understanding or for power. In oriental culture, the spiritual hierarchy is deterministic; the person positioned lower is central because he still has a lot to learn. He takes priority because he has the longest way to go. In occidental culture, the person positioned highest is central. Unfortunately not because he still has to learn a lot, but because he has power. Our structure hierarchy is based on a ranking of functional dependent responsibilities and we prefer to reward role-related behavior more than wisdom. Yet working high up in the hierarchy is just working high up in the hierarchy, because all the work needs to be done.

Managing one day a week is enough for first-line managers
The leader of a group of professionals can make his work a lot more pleasant if he concentrated his management work into one day a week, for instance, Monday. Given the burden of management, it is usually still necessary to spread the administrative hassle either by forming a daily committee or by appointing a sort of assistant who has had training in management stuff and can take on all the odd jobs related to time logging, money, and reports for "them upstairs." Such a person has a full-time job and reports to the first-line manager who, as a result, can spend four days a week on his discipline. Obviously the first-line manager also has regular R&D (result and development) sessions with the management person. Because this assistant is a subordinate, instead of being at an equal level, there is little risk that the assistant can build his own empire, if that is what he wants. It could be tempting with the boss spending four days a week in a white coat somewhere else. The construction sketched above has, for example, proven very effective in hospitals.

The other model I learned from the chairman of a university discipline group that consists of 45 employees. He has formed a daily (or executive) council – the DC – whose three members work in that capacity only on Mondays. Monday mornings, there are the formal group meetings about education and research and the DC decides on travel requests, purchasing of equipment, vacancies, profile sketches, room allocation, conflicts, etc. The professionals are not allowed to make any appointments, the doors have to be open and everyone is restricted to doing "light work" only, like filling out lists and reading. Monday afternoon everyone must be present, except in case of illness or foreign travel. Everyone can go to each other's rooms to get to know one another, brainstorm about new educational or research projects, to make appointments to form new coalitions, etc. Thus from Tuesday to Friday everyone is standard output focused, in the discipline group, in his own garden, in Las Vegas, you name it; including the DC members. The DC members demonstrate atypical behavior only on Mondays and to accentuate this they sport a baseball cap that says "management in action" on Mondays. At the end of the day they take off the caps and are again like everyone else. And the slogan for the management work is: "There is nothing in a university that cannot wait until Monday." If only a lot more organizations would say that!

Even more radical: professionals do not manage, not even one day!

"... and then they got themselves a manager," was the rather disrespectful title of a research report title that I (MW) wrote for the advisory group managers of a large consultancy. The problem was that, because of the administrative burden, these managers could not spend enough time in their profession and on the content of the work of their subordinates. Their work satisfaction had dropped considerably. When the consultancy was much smaller everything happened automatically but now there was also something else that required their attention. Problems about parking space, conflict in the secretarial office, brochures with funny colors, old IT equipment, protests against the new magazine procedure, endless talking about the layout of the annual report, and more of the same trivial stuff.

My advice was to appoint a sort of general manager who would take care of all the paperwork so that they all could concentrate on doing their work. The meeting of the management advisory group would appoint her – they preferred a woman – and can also terminate the contract. She should not be a consultant because then she would eventually get too involved in the content. Her tasks are external representation, communication, marketing and facilities management and, of course, she will make less money than an advisory group manager, because managing a secondary process is not really such a big deal. The advice was followed, the managing director has arrived, everything is working fine and all involved are concentrating on what they are good at.

In 1994, Hedlund formulated a number of concise characteristics of a modern knowledge-intensive organization:

- Putting things together, combining rather than dividing them
- Temporary constellations of people and units rather than permanent structures
- The importance of personnel at "lower" levels in inter-functional, interdivisional, and international dialogue, rather than handling coordination through managers and only at the top
- Lateral communication and dialogue rather than vertical
- Top-level management as catalyst, architect of communications (technical and human) and infrastructure, and protector of knowledge investment rather than monitor and resource allocator

- "Heterarchy" as the basic structure (a network of elements sharing common goals in which each element shares the same "horizontal" position of power and authority, each having an equal vote) rather than hierarchy

Do not manage based on process but on desired output: Do so with the aid of Personal and Team Commitment Statements

In the previous chapter, we mentioned that in the triple career ladder structure, the responsibility for efficiency lies with the management line. In Chapter 2, we argued that responsibility should be placed elsewhere. To our disappointment, we had to conclude in Chapter 1 that managers responsible for efficiency prefer to "operationalize" from the top down, with high frequency, inserting too many "vertical thermometers" into the work process. The bureaucracy this creates works counterproductive to achieving the desired operational excellence. It is a brilliant paradox: the more you want to plan and control efficiency, the less efficient the system becomes.

Scientists discover new element

Because it has no electrons, Bureaucratium is inert, it will react with nothing. Yet it can be chemically proven because all other reactions around it slow down. According to the scientists, a miniscule amount of Bureaucratium is sufficient to create a reaction that will take four days where normally it takes just one second. The life span of Bureaucratium is about three years. During that period it does not really decay but reorganizes, whereby assistant neutrons, vice neutrons and assistant vice neutrons change position. It has also been affirmed that the atom mass increases after each reorganization.
(Philips NatLab-Journal, 1991)

So the question arises: "What is the alternative to efficiency?" And the answer is to concentrate on the output and not on the throughput. Mind you, it is not about pre-defined results that need to be achieved with *the customer* (those are *outcomes* like "stay healthy," "no more stealing," "make more profit") but about effort commitments through which such *outcomes* become more deliberate and more plausible. The Personal Commitment Statements (PCSs) agreed with professionals provide a potentially successful tool for output-based management.

Manage based on output, unless ...

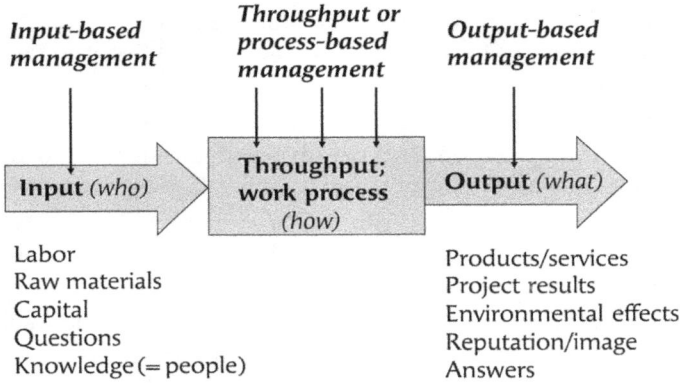

Input-based management	Throughput or process-based management	Output-based management

Input *(who)* → **Throughput; work process** *(how)* → **Output** *(what)*

Labor	Products/services
Raw materials	Project results
Capital	Environmental effects
Questions	Reputation/image
Knowledge (= people)	Answers

HOW = the functional autonomy of the knowledge worker
WHAT = the strategic autonomy of the manager, who says when it is ready and what it costs

Output-based management by using Personal Commitment Statements

In the "cookie factory," output-based management is controlled through the target-strategy hierarchy.

When the target is set at a certain hierarchical level (*What* do we want to achieve?), that same level determines the strategy (*How* to do it?).

That strategy has to be translated by the level below into measurable targets, and for the realization of those targets another strategy is formulated, which in turn is input for the level below, etc., until one finally arrives at the team that operates the cookie machine. Here's a simple example to clarify this. The management of the Cookies business unit has formulated its target for the next year: to reduce the production costs by 5% while retaining the same turnover. The strategy is: production improvement. The Luxury Cookies product group translates that strategy into the following target: increase productivity per full-time operator by 3% and reduce the downtime of the production machines also by 3%. The strategy of increasing operator productivity involves a slight reduction of the noon break and a slight increase in the speed of the machines. The strategy of reducing downtime is a further shift from curative to preventive maintenance of the production line, executed at night between midnight and 8 am. In a civilized factory with self-managing production teams, the operators and mechanics themselves can translate strategy into targets that they can accomplish at the workplace level. Such a hierarchically staged sequence of one-on-one translations of targets and strategies does not work in a knowledge-intensive organization. That has to do with the high level of dynamics in the development of the production factor knowledge (especially if one compares it with the development of the production factor labor) and, related to that, with the high level of unpredictability of interaction between cause and consequence.

A knowledge-intensive organization, contrary to the traditional production organization, knows too little deterministic causality to deal adequately with the target-strategy hierarchy. In a traditional factory things are relatively easy. A manager of Philips Lighting once told me (MW): "Look here; if you transport light bulbs, you transport mainly air. That is expensive, so you have to put the bulb factory near the customer; local for local. And then it is only a matter of efficiency: whoever has the fastest bulb line, has won."

Such algorithmic statements are rare for knowledge-intensive organizations. That is why it is more productive for knowledge-intensive labor to put more emphasis on qualitative – if you like, vague – notions, directions and intentions that could, for example, be part of a collective ambition (see Chapter 1). A collective ambition that is meaningful for both the highest and the lowest hierarchical level can be directly linked to knowledge at workplace level, by posing the following question: "What are your plans for next year to get closer to your organization's collective ambition?" And there it is: the justification and the essence of the Personal Commitment Statement.

The PCS-defined output has to be clearly formulated so that it will be possible to determine if it has been achieved or not, or only partly achieved. That is what is meant here by output-based management, contrary to results-based or outcome-based management. In the latter case, one usually assumes that the execution of a work process, when done correctly, *always* leads to the desired result with the customer, patient, or civilian; in the case of knowledge work, this is fiction. After all, the result does not show if someone has done a good job or not. A judge cannot guarantee that the sentenced criminal will not repeat his crime after he has done his time, a management consultant cannot promise a company that it will make more profit, and a cured patient can become ill again the next day.

Hence, in professional work, the relationship between the executed work process and the associated result is rather fuzzy. In addition to the fact mentioned in Chapter 1 that professionals are difficult to manage using "vertical rules and procedures," that vagueness provides all the more reason not to be too enthusiastic about process-based or throughput-based management.

Over two thousand years ago, ancient Greek philosophers agreed that medicine was a strange art. It was strange because, from the outcome, one could not tell whether one had done a good job. A doctor can treat a patient correctly but still see this patient die. On the other hand, another patient who has not been treated that well, not exactly according to the normal procedures, can make a full recovery.

The objective of medicine is the apparent restoration of health. That is why the Greeks, and after them the Romans, called it a "stochastic skill." We still use the word stochastic in our language, for instance, in the expression "a stochastic process." By that we mean a process that is subject to random events. This is contrary to a "deterministic process" in which doing A always results in B. The immediate consequence of accepting the stochastic element is that you cannot determine whether someone is a good or a bad doctor by checking if his patients get well. No, you need to check if he has done everything to facilitate recovery. This, in fact, shifts the objective of medicine. The objective is no longer to cure. The objective is to do everything possible to promote curing. The stoics used the analogy of the man who aims his arrow at a target. It is unimportant if he hits the target, because a sudden wind may occur and deflect the arrow. More important is that he aims at it in the right way.

The subject addressed here is better known in scientific circles as the effort commitment versus result commitment. The first can be achieved, the latter cannot. As a consequence, when formulating targets, it has to be about quantified and measurable direct results of executed work processes and not about the (social) effects of the results on the client, patient, or civilian. Hence, output-based management and not outcome-based or result-based management. So indeed, we have agreed with this scientist that he shall publish two articles a year in a double-blind reviewed international A or B magazine (but not that those articles will be read and cited or lead to new products or services). That indeed, we have agreed with the judge that this year he will produce N legal rulings but not that the people of New York should feel safer at the end of the year. Or we have agreed with the French teacher that this year he will achieve a pass result of P% but not that the students can speak understandable French on their next trip to France. You can ask a drilling supervisor to drill a well but you cannot ask him that the same well will produce more than 1000 barrels of oil a day, or even that he finishes the well to the required depth.

Long live the internet

A few years ago, I (CH) organized, in a capacity that you could call first-line drilling manager, a "wildcat" well on mainland Europe for a small independent oil exploration company in the US. The well had to be drilled in a geologically unknown area where no wells had been drilled before. All we had to go on was old 2D seismic images and some recent low frequency seismic images. I got the team together and made an initial budget that was thrown out by the CEO for being too high. He told the Exploration and Production VP that it had to be done cheaper. "Sharpen your pencil and see if we can do this for half the cost. If Cees' team is as good as you say it is, it should be possible." Against my better judgment, we lowered the budget substantially by taking a dodgy rig, applying borderline engineering standards, taking out all the contingencies and hoping we would be lucky. Wrong. Things were going very slowly mainly due to a combination of rig equipment breakdowns, the unexpected artesian water flows and the hardness of the formation. As a result, the well threatened to go over budget. Enter the internet. Thanks to the internet and keen service companies everyone can now get real-time information at his desk on all drilling parameters. The people who understand the intricacies of the drilling process don't use it and let the professionals get on with it. However, the less people know about drilling, the more they are inclined to use it, especially when things are not going well. Our CEO had no specialist petroleum engineering background and was looking at the screen all the time. Every time he felt that something was not normal he would storm out of his office and question the E&P VP about it. It was driving us to distraction and the atmosphere around the office got really bad. The CEO insisted to the VP that I should go to the rig site more often and "kick some ass." I told the VP, who had an engineering background, that that would not be necessary and that, in fact, it would be counterproductive. I had full faith in the specialists on the rig and if indeed they were doing a bad job (which I knew they were not) they should be replaced or should not have been there in the first place. These specialists had been on jobs worldwide for years and were seasoned professionals and there was no reason for me to go out there other than for scheduled visits. It would disturb the chain of command with them worrying about me being there rather than focusing on solving the problems at hand. The VP understood but to keep the peace he said I had to go there and "get things moving." One day, the drilling rig had a mechanical problem and we had to wait for spares. After a few days, I got an email directly from the CEO – jumping the chain of command – asking me why we were "still" not drilling. I answered back with an email saying that, as he knew, we had a mechanical problem with the rig. I went a bit further and suggested to him that he should leave it alone and give encouragement especially when things were going badly. People on the rig were suffering under this constant strain and lost motivation. Some of them quit. It became everyone for themselves with the predictable result. Process-based management in its purest and ugliest form.

Looking for a first violinist

The Amsterdam Concertgebouw Orchestra was looking for a first violinist. Part of the selection procedure was an audition. Because the audition was performed behind a screen, the judges could not see the candidate, did not know whether he was playing a Stradivarius or an ordinary violin, or whether he was holding the bow correctly, or if his body was moving the Italian way with the dramatic lines in the composition or whether he modestly let the music talk for itself, or whether his personal hygiene was within the acceptable limits, or whether there was any charisma, or whether it was a he or a she. It wasn't important for the judges to know such things. The only thing they would experience was the result: the musicality of the interpretation of the piece of music by the candidate. That way it was quite possible that one of the second violists of the orchestra was behind the screen. If the judges feel that "candidate number 3" produces the best sound and gives the most impressive interpretation, then he or she will advance in the procedure. The surprise afterwards that "candidate number 3" turns out to be one of their "team" does not weaken the decision. That is typically output-based management. Whether the critics or spectators will be moved by his playing (= outcome) we don't know yet. Neither do we know if his way of working (his approach) will lead to constructive collaboration with his colleagues (= the end result of ignoring throughput i.e. managing the working process).

Now we go to the technique of creating and working with Personal Commitment Statements.

Personal Commitment Statement (PCS) – WHAT?

What to do:
- the initiative to compose the content of the PCS lies with the professional;
  hence bottom-up, given the collective ambition [long-term reference] and the management letter for the current year [short-term reference]
- the PCS is determined in negotiations between employee and manager
- optimizing criteria thereby are: viability and challenge/ability
- content:
  - required outputs, in terms of production: billable days, innovations, new clients, border crossing collaborations, publications, training results, coaching of juniors, etc.
  - optional: agreements about indirect work within the framework of separating staff from administrative tasks
- duration: one year or six months

Within the framework of collective ambition and the annual framework letter – or a similar strategic document – each professional is requested which quantifiable and thus measurable goals he wants to achieve in the coming year. Examples: I will make D billable days this year, produce P infotainment programs for target group D, perform S cataract operations on patients with complication C, develop 3 computer games for girls aged between 10 and 12 years old, train 1 junior and coach 2 trainees, set up a cross-border collaboration program with department A or with company O, apply for a patent for principle P, develop 2 substances with super conductive properties based on an XY alloy, and so on.

Make sure that the objectives are measurable because otherwise it cannot be determined whether they were met or not, but do allow for defining on a high abstraction or aggregation level: "Something more like the CD," said the director of the Philips Research Lab in one of his New Year speeches.

The question of whether we can still talk about professionals is justified if the PCS goals (*what*) *can* be formulated so that, as a result, the freedom of the work process organization (*how*) is severely curtailed. Think about police officers with a target of writing tickets for an amount B in category C, or tax people that must find a correction in favor of the treasury to a minimum predetermined amount, per N checked declarations with difficulty level M. Both examples are based on statistically founded standards. Nothing is really wrong with those standards. However, the fact that statistics can be used to arrive at a quantifiable output per worker indicates predictable routine work: if you do *this*, sooner or later you always get *that* result, and as we have seen, for a professional that would be fiction.

A TCS – Team Commitment Statement – is made by ramming a staple through all PCSs of all the team members or as a team to take responsibility for a jointly composed task-defined TCS whereby the translation into what that TCS means for each team member individually, is implicit. Based on experiences and the actual team composition, the team considers it equally challenging and attainable to carry out the TCS they created together. In such a directly created TCS, i.e. without the basis of individual PCSs, there is a good chance that the team members feel responsible for each other's performance and are more prepared to help one another and take over each other's tasks if someone is ill or has family problems.

Team Commitment Statement (TCS) of medical institution M.

Essence:
- Agreements with the management about WHAT the institution will do in the coming planning period.
- HOW that is done is up to the competence of the team (functional autonomy).
- Frame of reference for the team: the collective ambition of the institution and the policy note for this year.
- Checking criteria: challenging but doable.
- A deal is a deal.

Content:
- *Quantitative targets:*

achievements per category, # publications, # training spots, agreements about how to improve the relationship direct/indirect personnel, waiting periods in the ER, how long are patients in, by type of disorder, etc.
- *Qualitative targets:*
  Skill improving activities, innovation (new protocols), organization intercollegial test, initiatives for multidisciplinary collaboration.

The TCS formulated in this way is then subjected to negotiations between professional (or the team delegation) and the first-line manager. The key is to test the TCS on attainability *and* its level of challenge. If, in the opinion of the manager, the TCS is not realistic within the given time frame and with the available means and yet he still signs off on it, the chances are that he will subject his people to too much stress or – even worse – burn-out. But if the TCS is not challenging enough and can be achieved lightly, then the organization will not "swing," there will be no energy, and boredom and apathy may strike.

The chance that the first-line manager can strike an optimum balance between challenge and realistic targets is a lot bigger if he comes from the ranks, has studied the profession, or has done the same work as the people that he now manages. For a "professional" manager (MBA, business economist) or generalist (psychologist, sociologist, or lawyer with a management degree) it will be far more difficult to set realistic and challenging targets within the expertise of the professional.

It is even more difficult for a lay manager to assess if the produced results meet the given specifications. That is why this type of manager always tries to escape into process management (= throughput-based management). If you don't know what it is about, then you go and check if people are at work on time, or don't go home too early, if they can distinguish between cost line items, line types, if they sit correctly at their desks, if they sign off on things in time. What else is there to do?

Henry Mintzberg put it brilliantly in the *Harvard Business Review*: "Managing without an intimate understanding of what is being managed, is an invitation to disharmony." It does not always apply, but it is always there ready to strike.

Another argument that promotes using expert first-line managers comes from Mihaly Csikszentmihalyi, professor in psychology at the Claremont Graduate University and inventor of the concept "flow." Flow is a very extreme state of consciousness whereby you get the feeling that everything is good and goes by itself, almost automatic and effortless. You are one with your work (a sort of symbiosis) and you forget time and your personal upkeep. Everyone has experienced that pleasant productive state at some point. Musicians say that they are "in the groove" and athletes call it being "in the race."

According to Csikszentmihalyi flow can only occur in the zone where the task and the required knowledge (= information x experience x skill x attitude) achieve equilibrium. If you have more knowledge than you can use, you get bored, "Under-used, over-managed!" says the professional. If you have too little knowledge there is anxiety.

It is impossible for a flow experience to occur in a state of boredom or anxiety. If you want your people to work with pleasure and high productivity – and who doesn't – then you must give them tasks in their "flow-zone." It then follows that the chance that a non-hands-on manager makes more mistakes in allocating tasks with flow potential, is much greater than a hands-on manager.

Professionals want to work in their "flow zone."

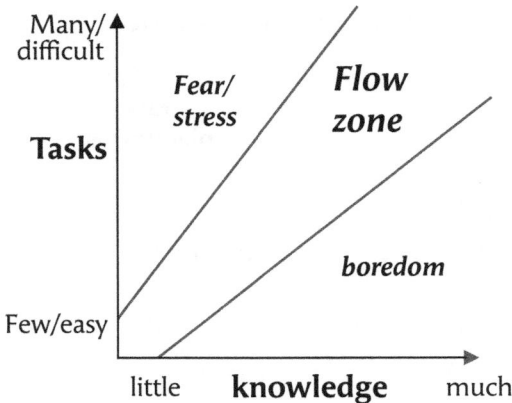

HOW the professional achieves his agreed PCS depends on his competence. The responsibility for that lies with the self-managing professional or team in case of a TCS. Asking every week or – even worse – every day how things are going, leans towards process-based management and, hence, needs to be avoided. The basis must be: "No news is good news." If the professional says nothing, it means that everything is going the right way. If he has judged wrongly (e.g. too optimistic), if there are obstacles, if there are unforeseen show stoppers and hurdles on the way, then the professional will flag this in the hope of finding a new solution together. Of course, it is great if the manager shows regular interest in the work of the professional, and even better if the professional regularly shares his enthusiasm about the interim results with his supervisor. That has nothing at all to do with process management. Furthermore, this year's PCS is a function of last year's (if it was too challenging last year, do a bit less this year. If it was too easy last year, do a bit more this year), and as such forms the basis for assessments and staff reports.

Differentiate in management style with the help of the PCS
With the help of Goold and Campbell (1987), it is possible to define output review, strategic coordination and operational planning & control.

Three Basic Management Styles

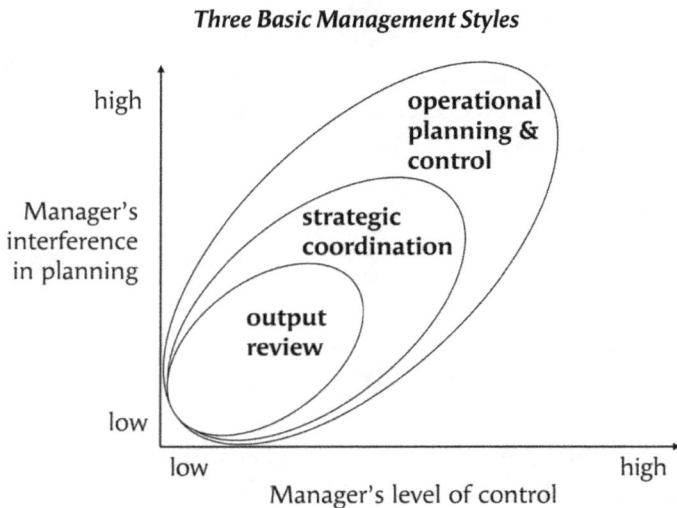

Output review:
Planning: the professional proposes his PCS; the proposal is on the basis of equality between professional and manager, is adapted where necessary, and then finalized.

Control: the first-line manager assesses afterwards if the outputs agreed and specified in the PCS have been met on time and on budget.

Strategic coordination:
Planning: the first-line manager gives in advance some guidelines which the professional has to take into account when creating his PCS. Of course, those guidelines have to do with the output (how, the work process). When negotiating the PCS, the supervisor checks if the guidelines have been addressed sufficiently.

Control: the first-line manager determines afterwards and interim at strategic moments selected by him if the results agreed in the PCS are or will be achieved on time, on budget, and, where applicable, in accordance with the agreed approach.

Operational planning and control:
Planning: the first-line manager proposes the PCS in which both the achievable results are defined (what) as well as by and large in what way these results can be achieved (how). The PCS will be finalized and firmed up by the manager after discussion with the professional.

Control: the supervisor follows the realization of the PCS on a periodic basis (per week, per month) and, based on his findings, he continuously gives suggestions with regard to the way in which the specified results have to be accomplished.

If this concerns directing teams of professionals, the word PCS must be replaced by TCS (Team Commitment Statement) and "professional" by "team leader" or "group leader."

Assuming that in the ideal situation, the professional and the first-line manager are most satisfied if the strategic autonomy (What to do) lies with the manager and the operational autonomy (how to do it) with the professional, then the preferred style of management is: output review. If the professional or the team in question has potentially the joy or sorrow of showing substantial synergy with one or more other professionals or teams, or if the situation is as such that the output of professional A in team A is a certain input for the work of worker B in team B, then the strategic coordination is with the lowest placed manager to whom the interacting professionals or teams report. If the professional or the team is seen seriously lacking in realizing the PSC or TSC during the recent planning period, then that worker or that team will in the next period be subjected to operational planning and control. Let's not be too difficult and only speak of "seriously lacking" if more than 20% of the agreed results have not been achieved. Obviously, this concerns a dimension that has to be measured based on experience because an objective measuring device for knowledge work does not exist. Certain tasks are obviously more difficult than others, there could be unexpected windfalls and setbacks, a scarcity of experts or machines have disappeared or are occupied at crucial moments, etc. The decision rules for making a choice between the three management styles are summarized below.

When and which management style to apply?

	IF the agreed targets are met. (>80%)	IF the agreed targets are not met. (>20%)
IF the unit * has substantial synergy or essential input-output interaction with other units	then: **STRATEGIC COORDINATION**	then always: **OPERATIONAL PLANNING & CONTROL**
IF the unit * is stand alone	then: **OUTPUT REVIEW**	

* a unit is a knowledge worker with a PCS or a team with a TCS

Now we can define the following rules for the introduction of a PCS/TCS practice with the corresponding differentiation on management styles:

1. Upon introduction of PCSs/TCSs, the first-line manager uses during the initial planning period the preferred management style for each unit (individual or team): output review.
2. The following is determined in mutual consultation between manager and unit at the end of the planning period:
   – to what degree the agreed targets have been met
   – how major deviations (>20%) from the set targets can be explained.
3. Depending on the result of step 2, the manager decides on the management style that he will use during the coming period with regard to the particular unit: again output review or strategic coordination, or operational planning & control.
4. Repeat step 2 and 3 again and again.

What follows is a somewhat stylized example of a faculty chairman who leads a group of scientists as a first-line manager. The targets that have to be met by most of them are clear:

1. Per subject, a score given by the students of >7 with a small standard deviation (the final score is a weighted average of the evaluation scores for the content of the lectures, presentations, study material, practical classes, exams, etc. What constitutes a "small standard deviation" can be determined on a case-by-case basis by the manager himself).
2. Two contributions to the national social debate recognizable for everyone, such as writing an opinion article in a national newspaper, or participating in a forum, or sitting on a panel at conferences and symposiums, attending a current affairs program on radio or TV.
3. Run a website that addresses a relevant issue, etc. (plus a few more specific targets with regards to graduates, PhDs and 2nd and 3rd tier funding research).

If an employee actually achieves these targets, then he is entitled to output review and he will only be required to be at the faculty on Monday mornings to attend the fixed meetings about education and research. And Monday afternoon everyone must be there to make "New Combinations" and do "light work" – for instance, reading – with the door open so that colleagues feel free to walk in for help with a problem, to brainstorm on the set-up of a new research study, for peer advice about reprogramming a lecture, etc. Should the employee be unable to attend on Monday, then he has to report that to the faculty chairman. The validity of the absence is checked against its importance (a conference in Boston, the birth of a child, moving house). The faculty management does not need to know where an employee who reaches his targets is from Tuesday to Friday – at home, working, or sitting in the garden – because for a successful scientist the only thing that counts is output-based management. An employee who has not reached his targets is expected to be at the faculty every day before 9 am and stay there until 5 pm. For him, operational planning & control is the management style that fits best, in which case physical presence helps. You can walk in easily, make short notice appointments, give feedback and so on. So in the case of output review, one can "buy" freedom by being basically "good." Protocols, guidelines and rules are particularly relevant for those who are not "good"(anymore), those who do not meet the targets (anymore).

Hence, a broad spectrum of management styles is expected from the first-line manager. He must be able to differentiate between individuals and teams (from 9 am to 10 am meet with team T in a strategic coordinating style, between 10 am and 11 am progress review with professional P in the operational & control style, etc.). He must be able to differentiate over time with regard to the same person or team. ("The last planning period I used the output review style for professional K. However, given his disappointing performance, I feel obliged in the coming period to exercise operational planning & control.")

The recommendation enthusiastically presented here to differentiate within one group between management styles for roughly the same type of professionals, stands in stark contrast with the management styles that are based on opinions such as, "What's good for the goose is good for the gander" and "What is good for Peter, must be good for

Paul." Those opinions are very relevant at the "cookie factory." Places where people cannot influence speed and quality, because people's hands must follow the machines. At the cookie factory, it would be unfair to give one person half the bonus when the other gets the full bonus, or to grant one worker a longer tea break than the other. But professionals can influence the quality and the pace of their work and therefore Galjaard's – professor in human genetics at Erasmus University, Rotterdam – proposition applies here: "Nothing is more unfair than the treatment of non-equals." We are all equal as humans but we differ in our knowledge (quality) and motivation (pace) and in knowledge-intensive organizations one can do relatively little to neutralize those differences. That is why first-line managers need to differentiate in their management style based on the results of the professionals entrusted to them and, on the other hand, professionals have a right to that differentiation.

A few ways how first-line managers can differentiate:

- Offer the knowledge worker the prospect of a place (or not) on the professional line of the dual or triple ladder (See Chapter 3)
- Offer (no) extra capacity in the form of assistants in training, pre-graduates, etc.
- Increase (decrease) secretarial capacity
- Make available a multi-window office or banish him to a one-window office (with a bad view)
- Schedule machine time, OT slots, etc. at attractive (bad) times on the roster
- Increase (decrease) the personal budget for travel to conferences (e.g. to Paris)
- Offer state-of-the-art IT (the latest this and that) versus "You better make do with what you've got."
- An (un)attractive parking spot
- Give more money vs. decrease the rate of a salary raise
- Give exemption from participation in boring committees vs. proposing him for participation in such committees

Finally, an example that shows why it makes good sense to let good professionals decide *how* they can do their work best and to leave process management for them out of the equation, at least for now. Moreover, the experience knowledge that seasoned professionals implicitly use is as elusive as it is explicable for planning & control-driven managers and their vertical management systems. Managers who have not come up the ranks are therefore particularly prepared to dismiss that experiential knowledge as completely irrelevant:

"Look here professor, we have never seen the gentlemen who take those decisions here on site," said the operator resentfully, as we toured the plant and stopped for a moment at an enormous vessel that was hissing and puffing. The spaghetti of pipes, vessels and valves made a big impression on me. "They simply sit in their offices behind their desks and decide on the basis of lots of paperwork that we in the control room have to reduce the number of operators during certain periods from two to one. Because you are then on your own you cannot make rounds through the plant. Now with two, we can still do that every four hours." Defending the client for a moment I explain that the operating rooms are so well designed and fitted with so many early warning systems, double checks and automatic safety systems that it should be safe. "Sure, the new control room is much better, much safer than the old one, but all these little gauges don't tell us everything. Take for instance last week. All gauges for the N3 were green but it was a bit of a – how shall I put it – strange combination of values. In any case, I had the feeling that something was not right and my colleague had the same feeling when I told him. When I started my round, I went straight to the N3 where I heard a funny knocking in the HFC valve. After some investigation we found out what it was and that way me and my buddy have probably avoided a nasty problem. You cannot hear the strange knocks in the control room, but the boys in the office do not know that. All they think of is efficiency. They hear nothing. They don't even listen!"

The "Ten commandments" of Dr. Gilles Holst, founder of the Philips Research lab.

1. Employ clever researchers, as young as possible, but with experience in academic research.
2. Do not pay too much attention to the details of the work they have done.
3. *Give employees much freedom and accept their idiosyncrasies.*
4. Let them publicize and partake in national and international activities.
5. Avoid a too strict organization. Let authority be driven by real knowledge.
6. Do not divide a laboratory by disciplines – mathematics, physics,

chemistry, etc. – but form multi-disciplinary teams.

7. Give great freedom in the choice of the work, but let the leaders in particular be conscious of their responsibilities with regards to the company.
8. Budget an industrial laboratory not by project and do not allow manufacturing departments to get budget say-so over research programs.
9. Promote the transfer of good older researchers from the laboratory to development and production in the factories.
10. Let the choice of subject also be decided by the standard of the academic science.

5 PEOPLE

Offer professionals continuous learning opportunities to ensure state-of-the-art involvement in their discipline

"The increase in the number of biomedical publications since 1870 has been exponential. (...) An estimated two million articles are published in biomedical journals each year. For a physician to read everything of possible biomedical relevance, it would be necessary to read about 6,000 articles a day."

If you make a quick calculation you see that that includes weekends. "Yes, but in my profession things are not moving as fast as in medical technology," you could say. OK, if we correct this with a factor of 10 that is still 600 articles per day. "And those academics must continue to publicize to make a career – *publish or perish* – and hence they often write variations on the same theme under another title." OK, let's make another downward correction with a factor of 10, and it *still* is 60 articles a day.

That is the problem with eternally aging professional knowledge. **Can we keep up?**

To be able to better quantify that aging, our colleague Den Hertog has, when he was in a creative mood, linked the expression "half value time" (or "half-life") known from physics or medicine, to knowledge. In simple term, this concept in physics indicates how long it takes for radioactive material to lose half of its radiation power. Den Hertog found that the relevant knowledge of an electrical engineer around 1987 did reduce by 50% in 10 years and 10 years later, in 1997, it took only five years. Half of the engineers who graduated in 2000, at the age of 22, had by 2005 (age 27) lost half of their knowledge, and in 2010 (age 32) will have only a quarter of the relevant knowledge he had as a student.

* Verhoeven, 1999

Taking this engineer as a benchmark for your own performance, you can estimate roughly what the situation is with regards to your own half value time.

Due to the ever diminishing half value time of knowledge (and especially technological knowledge), the knowledge life cycle also gets ever shorter. Based on that perception, we can give the following definition of a knowledge worker: a knowledge worker is someone who, in order to execute his primary task, must be able to learn a lot both *permanently* and *relatively* (relative compared to bus drivers, barkeepers, football players, and other skilled workers who mainly try to practice a certain routine skill more effectively and more efficiently). Because the surrounding in which the knowledge worker operates is dynamic by definition, he has to keep learning to maintain his knowledge to stay context-relevant, with learning as the production process that turns out knowledge.

Although knowledge in itself cannot age, it must be obvious that by "old knowledge" we mean knowledge that at this moment in time is not suited to solve present problems. For instance, because new knowledge has been developed to tackle those questions and problems better, faster, cheaper, easier, more pleasantly, or more durably. Often it is the wealth of potential applications that determines if knowledge should be considered obsolete. That is why knowledge about the workings and use of the steam engine remains relevant for someone that teaches the history of technology.

There are at least two causes for knowledge aging faster: first, the dramatic increase in the pace of technological progress (IT, internet, Challenger) and second globalization means knowledge is no longer judged from a local perspective. All knowledge *is* universal. The norm has become absolute: the benchmark is the latest knowledge in a particular field, wherever you are.

"Doctor, do you know about the thesis of John Abernathy who got his PhD last week in London?"

A friend recently told me the story of a well educated young woman who had to undergo surgery. The operation was routine so the chance of complications was less than 4%. The patient had enthusiastically searched the internet in the run-up to the operation to gather more information about the things to come. In doing this, she hit on something that was in her view very interesting and relevant to her case. She made an appointment with the surgeon to discuss this. It is the bane of all professionals: the patient, client, customer, or citizen with an internet extract. You have to explain again that there is no quality control on internet content, that any quack can publish anything he likes and so on, that good doctors have no time to play with the internet, etc. But this lady asked him: "Doctor, do you know about the thesis of John Abernathy who last week was awarded his PhD in London?" No I don't. "His doctoral thesis was on a small clamp, and he claims that with that clamp you can half the chance of complications, so from 4% to 2%. You really should know about this thesis." "Well," the surgeon answered, "it has probably slipped past me, but next week both the next *Lancet* and the *New England Journal of Medicine* will be published and if it really is important then it will be mentioned in there. Moreover, in three weeks we have our big international "small clamp conference" and if this is really important, this Abernathy will certainly be there and I will take the chance to have a word with him about it." But he could see that the answer did not completely satisfy her, and so he added something that usually comes in handy in this kind of situation: "But we also have those innovative little clamps." "Show them to me," she responded. Normally, he would not consent to such a request, but he thought maybe it has something to do with knowledge management. Why don't I go along with this; could be an excuse to open a bottle of wine with Weggeman. And so he took her to the operating theatre, opened the instrument cabinet and pointed at a funny shaped instrument with levers. "Next month we will operate on you using that very clamp." "It does not look anything like it!" said the young woman self assured. "What does the Abernathy clamp look like then?" he asked, whereupon she took a print of it from her handbag. Now the doctor patient relation became a bit "square" and he pressed a button to make his beeper go off. "Sorry, madam, emergency. It is your choice: next month you are here as planned or you make an appointment in London with that jolly little clamp." He shook her hand and walked down the corridor. After a few steps a smile came to his face. "What I really should have said: why don't you go and have a look around in Vladivostok; they also write very nice articles there."

This is an example of – if you like – the over-informed citizen, patient, or customer who confronts the professional with what CNN would call "the latest" in the trade. The customer cannot apply the knowledge because of a lack of skill and the necessary infrastructure, but he knows that the knowledge is there and expects experts to be familiar with it and also apply this knowledge.

In addition, the customer has two competitive advantages over the knowledge worker: the customer has both time and focus. He is at a given moment only interested in a small part of sub-specialization of the broad repertoire that the knowledge worker has to keep up with. Moreover, the customer has all the time in the world to search long and deep for relevant information and he does that with almost the same IT and in the same database as the professional. In addition, the customer can increasingly better judge the information on quality and relevance because he is increasingly better educated (about 35% of young people are in higher education and projections for 2020 shows that figure will rise to about 50%). That is why more and more people are able to give a rational interpretation of abstracts taken from the internet and international scientific articles. Hence, it is more and more difficult to fool the client, customer, patient, or citizen, to send him on a wild goose chase or to dismiss him with an arrogant reference to one's own (obsolete) experience, when the real reason is lack of state-of-the-art expertise.

- "Yes madam, I know about that new material, but the expansion coefficient is not yet within the required bandwidth."
- "That method is being applied in the US, but the results are problematic which is why we do not use it here in Europe."
- "That is indeed a promising new technique you mention but it is still in its infancy. Moreover, we can achieve the same thing with traditional methods."
- Cheeky proposition: "You really have searched the internet thoroughly, but don't you think that if it would work we would have introduced it ourselves?"

And many more of these kinds of rationalizations and excuses that impress customers increasingly less, thank God.

Knowledge is defined here as the – partly unconscious – ability someone has to execute a task. An ability that is a metaphoric function of the Information, the Experience, the Skills and the Attitude that someone owns at a given moment: $K = f(I^*ESA)$.

If knowledge is the ability that enables someone to execute a given task and if "giving meaning to data" is a task, then you assign that meaning with the help of the knowledge that you have at that moment in time. That way knowledge becomes dynamic: knowledge is used to generate more knowledge from data. That newly created knowledge reacts with the existing information, experience, skills and attitude and thus new knowledge is formed.

Dynamic Knowledge

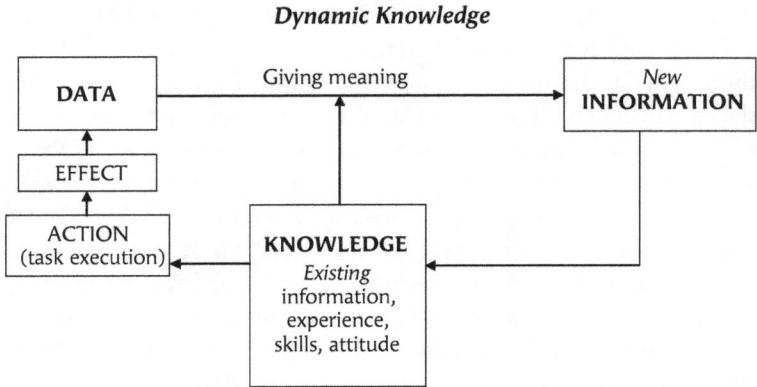

Hence, knowledge is the ability to enable someone to execute a given task by task related selection, interpretation and appreciation of present data so that new task-relevant information results.

For that selection, interpretation and appreciation of data, theoretical knowledge ("old" information) or practical familiarity (experience) is needed with the domain in which the task takes place, or with the processes (skills) that are relevant to the execution of the given task.

The attitude determines whether the professional has the least interest in studying newly available data to turn it into information. Hence, the attitude drives the personal knowledge renewal and the above quotes are illustrative of the attitude that can best be compared with an idling engine: new data offered by customer or colleague is given little or no significance. Thus, the knowledge does not mutate and you stay where you were while wasting energy.

What is frustrating about the ever faster aging of knowledge is that it is mainly caused by just one of the four components of knowledge: information. The longer you live, the more you have a richly filled personal database with experiences that is accessible via your memory. You could see it this way: your memory acts like a search engine consulting the experience database and then it gets and proposes those experiences that are relevant to the execution of the task. The larger the database, the more successful the memory will be in finding something relevant.

With the exception of motor skills, most other skills improve the longer you live, as long as you practice them. The longer you are in France the better you speak French. By the same token, there are very few people who play the piano every day for two hours who do not end up playing better. Finally, the attitude: the "basic beliefs" with their standards and values crystallize out the older you get and then others qualify that attitude increasingly in terms such as equilibrium, harmony, wisdom, etc. The only component that erodes is: information. That is where the 6,000 medical articles a year and the "Abernathy's small clamp" come in. Can you not compensate for that erosion with extra experience or skills? Not according to famous neuroscientists like Dennett and Damasio: there is no plus sign between the 4 components but multiplication signs instead. Knowledge = Information x Experience x Skills x Attitude.

The high development pace of knowledge – mainly technological and sociocultural – causes many professionals to be "obsolete" long before they reach sixty. A standard escape for the knowledge worker is to escape into management. Not a bad idea because the half value time for management knowledge is about 2,000 years. Indeed, a gigantic number of management books and articles are being continuously produced; however new data is few and far between. Should there be a semblance of a new finding, then it is often about something known but under a different name, or it simply isn't true. Hence, there is little reason to attack all those pages with so-called management innovations and paradigm shifts. It suffices sometimes to read a small book or article to keep up with the ever-continuing development of professional jargon.

"A lot of what is new is not correct and a lot of what is correct is not new."

Management is not a profession, it is an occupation

THEN: (Old wine)	NOW: (New bottle)
organizational change	transformation
culture change	mindset change
efficiency improvement	business process redesign
performance indicators	balanced scorecard
function appraisal	360° feedback
managing professionals	knowledge management
distrust	making transparent
project proposal	value proposition
project proposition	business case
first impression	quick scan
re-structuring; down-sizing	link active consequences to the sailing regatta.

In short: a manager who continuously improves his skills through practice and who has made a habit of reflecting on his experiences does not go "stale." The sea of concepts, methods, and techniques that they pour on themselves – with the help of an army of advisors and consultants – contains mostly cosmetic innovations. That is why, as far as new management methods and techniques are concerned, the information component is not that important for the professional knowledge of the manager. When I ask you to imagine a good manager and I ask you then why this is such a good manager, you will probably mention his vast experience. There is even more chance that you will talk about his skills: his analytical skills, his social and communication skills, his intuition and powers of imagination, his creative skills, and so on. But you will probably talk most about his attitude, his values and standards, his integrity and fairness, his approach. Rarely will you say: I think he is a very good manager because he reads the *Harvard Business Review* and uses whatever is in it.

To go into management when you can't cut it anymore as a professional is an effective strategy (if you have the necessary skills and a fitting attitude), but we have to be careful that that option is only open to few, because otherwise an even larger management density will emerge than we already have at our knowledge-intensive organizations. And nobody needs that. Managers cost lots of money and their added value is rather limited.

The manager: big torch, little light

Three bricklayers are working at the same building site. An organizational sociologist who performs field work as part of a motivation study asks all three what they are doing. "I'm stacking up bricks with cement in between; that way they stick together better," says the first. "I'm making a low wall between the centre aisle and a side aisle," says the second. Then the third bricklayer, who is doing exactly the same work as the others, answers: "I'm building a cathedral!" That is the mission driven expert; that is what we need: cathedral builders!

Three smartly dressed gentlemen are looking on: the architect who is proud of the high artistic level of his design, the builder who with the latest planning and control system will make sure that the project will stay within budget, and the developer who has scraped together the required funds using a smart financing structure.

The bricklayer does not care. He knows full well that without masonry there will not be a cathedral. And while he stacks one brick on another, he gets this wonderful thought: "Masonry is completely different from talking about masonry."

Knowledge workers must work shorter instead of longer!
In the knowledge economy, things work differently than in the factories and offices of the industrial economy. Experience and technical skills are the most important thing for the employees of those traditional organizations. And the longer you work, the more experience you get. The same goes for skills. If you just keep applying them, they will develop further. If you keep the workers of those offices and factories working longer, they can also capitalize on their ever-increasing experience and skills. The chance that their productivity grows the older they get, is then indeed high. The only thing is that there are increasingly fewer factories and offices where people are more or less working routinely to do the same work progressively better and more efficiently. Only in industries like agriculture, transport, catering, construction, and behind the counters of banks and public services can we potentially make more money by having people work longer because people retire later.

However, that logic does not apply to the modern knowledge-intensive organization. There, we find employees to whom new information is equally if not more important than experience and skill. Many of those jobs begin with an "a": architects, advisors, accountants, anesthetists, attorneys, Afghanistan experts, and so on. Such people dominate our knowledge economy and their number is rapidly increasing. They have to keep learning to be good at their jobs relative to, for example, truck drivers, bakers, plumbers, and production line workers. It requires reading professional literature, attending seminars and conferences, participating in training sessions and study sessions, being prepared to learn from younger people and to deal with innovations that customers, citizens and patients have found on the internet. Research shows that the motivation of knowledge workers to keep abreast of the latest developments decreases with age. It is not that the learning skills get less, but it is more mental fatigue: "Do we have to change again?" "Do these changes never stop?" And because knowledge ages relentlessly faster, fatigue strikes ever earlier. For designers of internet related software and for nano and bio technologists it can happen at 35, for electrical engineers and tax lawyers five to ten years later. It means that more knowledge workers than before are less good at an earlier age. To have knowledge workers work to a higher age ultimately leads to people using old know-how. The surgeon, who has not learned to treat "endoscopically," keeps making large incisions. That increases trauma and implies longer recuperation for the patient, a need for more capacity, and a greater demand on personnel. All that increases the costs.

Another example is from 12 years ago. I (MW) had read somewhere that amalgam fillings could emit mini-volts that under certain circumstances could influence tiny electric currents in the brain. So I asked my dentist to fill that new cavity in my tooth with epoxy or ceramic material. He did not like my interfering with his business at all. "Sir, that technique is in its infancy. We cannot yet sufficiently control the shrinking and expansion of these substances." Later I understood what was going on here. My dentist was 54 at the time and was more involved in building his second house in Spain than with keeping up with innovations in his profession. He had used amalgam for 30 years and did not see why he could not continue using it until his retirement.

Allowing professionals to continue working to an older age can lead to many more instances like this in our knowledge economy. As the populate ages, we will see more and more knowledge workers "coasting" on the methods that they have already mastered, leaving the innovations in their profession for what they are. The result is that patients, customers and citizens receive outdated products and services that have alternatives that are cheaper, faster and more accurate, safer, more effective, healthier, easier, and user friendlier. The social costs of this professional conservatism are gigantic.

To have older professionals work to an older age is penny wise and pound foolish

Paul Scheffer, professor of European studies at Tilburg University, asserts that if all people above 55 were to stop working that would mean "destruction of social capital." That indeed applies to artesian work such as glass blowing, sheep shearing, and violin building, and also for some of the "cookie factories," but does not apply at all to knowledge workers. To force knowledge workers to work longer only makes sense if they are obliged to stay "up to date" in their profession. That implies studying until an older age and making time available to promote expertise. To keep knowledge workers employed, without sending them back to school, is, on balance, expensive. It is penny wise and pound foolish.

Professionals must continue to learn a lot if they are to continue to exercise their profession. The learning pressure used to be a lot lower in the old days. Maintaining a high learning level in the first 30 years formed the basis for another 30 years of capitalization of that knowledge. By the time that knowledge became obsolete or redundant, retirement age had arrived and the knowledge worker could concentrate on having a good time or convalesce, whatever seems more appropriate.

As a result of the ever-decreasing half value time, the knowledge worker reaches the end of his professional career at an ever younger age. IT professionals who prefer to make longer hours instead of taking the time to learn explicitly about state-of-the-art developments, or doctors who continue to use partly dated techniques rather than taking some time off to study newly available medical knowledge, will have to admit when they reach 35 or 40, that this approach has brought them dangerously close to the category "storytellers" (see the diagram below).

At one time, I (MW) advised a government ministry in the Netherlands on a mid-life study for medical specialists in which they would re-enter university part-time for a period of one to two years at the age of 40. That was not such a bad idea; moreover, thanks to the patient waiting lists in hospitals, dated knowledge of older specialists in the Netherlands is not really an issue. My proposal died due to a lack of funds: who will pay for that? In what proportion do we need to charge the specialist, the hospital he works in, the insurance and the government? Blah blah blah.

Due to the ever shorter half value time of knowledge,
we will become less good at what we do at an ever younger age
– that is, if we don't do anything

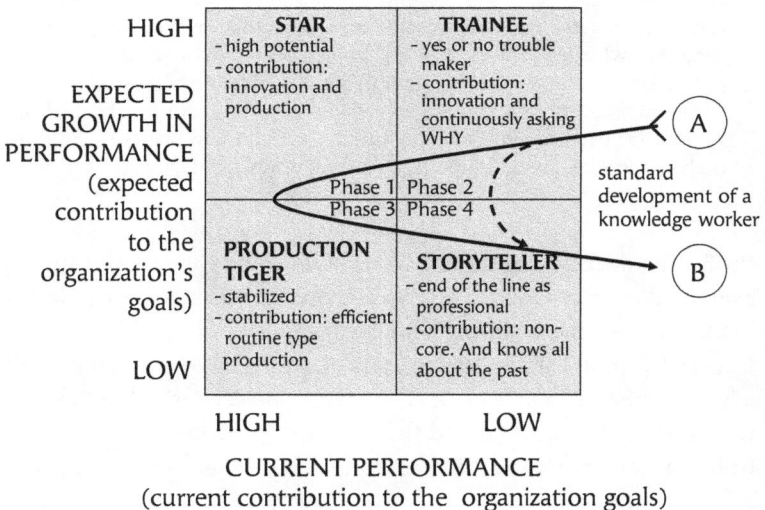

	STAR	TRAINEE
HIGH	- high potential - contribution: innovation and production	- yes or no trouble maker - contribution: innovation and continuously asking WHY

EXPECTED GROWTH IN PERFORMANCE (expected contribution to the organization's goals)

Phase 1 | Phase 2
Phase 3 | Phase 4

	PRODUCTION TIGER	STORYTELLER
LOW	- stabilized - contribution: efficient routine type production	- end of the line as professional - contribution: non- core. And knows all about the past

A

B

standard development of a knowledge worker

HIGH   LOW

CURRENT PERFORMANCE
(current contribution to the organization goals)

As this diagram shows, the standard development of a professional is as follows: you enter an organization as a trouble maker (or not). The contribution to the realization of the organization's goals is at that moment still limited, but a lot of growth is expected, otherwise you would not have been hired. In the second phase, you (may) become a star or have high potential. The actual performance is already high and further growth is expected. Then you become a production tiger. That category often forms the backbone of a company. The growth is gone but the contribution to the realization of the organization's goals remains high and relevant. Production tigers keep "digging trenches" and "thread pearls," are generally very loyal, and suffer under a lack of management attention. If the production tiger does nothing (meaning: does not invest in a new focus on his talents) he lands in the category of storytellers: the growth has already gone, now the relevance of the actual contribution goes down as well. Storytellers have arrived at the end of their career, they know everything of times gone by and like to talk about that at great length. The dotted line indicates the recruitment and selection errors. People that have to take that short cut from trainee to storyteller, do not take part in the festivity sketched above.

In the days of our parents, when the half value time of knowledge was not that short, you ended up – depending on your discipline – in the BS category around the age of 60. That was not too bad. You could hear younger colleagues say: "Oh well, he is 'fading out' a bit" or: "No problem, we can make him a coach or mentor or something equally vague" or: "We can see the vacancy coming already" or: "He is already following a course on 'what to do after retirement.'" Today's knowledge workers however are – depending on their discipline – already finished at 35, 40, or 45, and 20 years "fading out" is just too expensive. So what can you do? One of the things that you can do is to apply a T-profile in the production tigerphase.

Dare to choose a T profile in time!
The T profile (T-shape profile) was introduced by Hans Weijers, CEO at Akzo-Nobel and former minister for economic affairs in the Netherlands. Key in this is that a knowledge worker in the third phase of his development, reduces his professional repertoire by selecting one specialty that he wants to master intensely (the vertical line of the T) and selects one to three adjacent areas (along the horizontal line of the T) that he wants to keep up with so that he can continue to communicate with his colleagues over the breadth of the profession. It is clear that the chance that you can keep up to date for many years with a small repertoire is higher than with a broad repertoire. The Ever-

lasting Man of All Seasons and The Ever Clever Jack of All Trades are implausible phenomena in today's knowledge economy.

The vertical line of the T demands that you choose a super-specialized area that is small enough for you to continue to be state-of-the-art for a long time. The horizontal line of the T prevents you from becoming a "tunnel nerd" who can only talk about *that* substance at *that* temperature and *that* pressure. The disciplines that you maintain at appreciable level in the cross on the T make sure that you can keep communicating about your discipline with other professionals that have in the vertical line of the T what you have got in the horizontal line.

Obviously such discipline boundary-breaking communication is indispensible in finding New Combinations (= innovation). You can also see it as follows: at the beginning of your professional life cycle, you can represent the width and depth of you knowledge in the form of a rectangle. In later phases of your career, when you threaten to become a storyteller, you cut from the bottom left and right two rectangulars with knowledge from the original large rectangular so that you are left with a T.

All sorts of variations are possible. A deep, thin vertical and a short horizontal: the super specialist. A short vertical and a long broad horizontal, the generalist, etc.

When I (MW) reached the age of 50, I made a T profile for myself. I decided to be good in the area of organizing and managing knowledge-intensive organizations; in the strongly related discipline area of innovation management and counseling. The latter was the discipline with the help of which I apply the two other disciplines. In my horizontal line I put culture change and philosophical aspects of management. I cut out: project management, program management, operations management (workflow control, process management, etc.), general organizational knowledge and a few sub areas. I took the books on those subjects to the university and placed them in the student library, I put the related old-fashioned plastic view graphs in the garbage and I put the PowerPoint presentations in the Windows recycle bin. I kept all those books for three weeks in my office, I did not throw away the garbage bag and I did not empty the recycle bin. It was quite something for me to dispose so rigorously of those physical props of my knowledge. It takes a certain amount of courage. And you ask yourself whether you have made the right choice. Hence the title of this section, **"Dare to choose for a T profile in time!"** In the fourth week I finally bit the bullet and kicked everything out, and since then I have no idea if I can continue to be a good professional in the disciplines in the vertical line of my T until I'm 60 years old.

In the addendum to this chapter you will find a detailed description of how to compose T profiles for your organization.

T-PROFILE
To avoid personal tunnel vision due to super-specializing

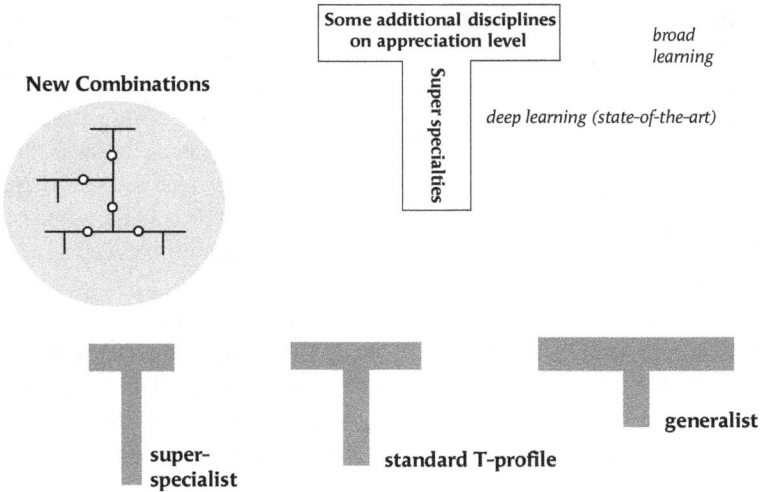

When it comes to knowledge management we are great proponents of collaborative structures, alliances, consortiums, and mergers because the bigger the organization, the more T profile super-specialties one can afford, the higher the level of discipline experience can stay.

An example: two regional hospitals are going to merge. Both have a stomach and intestinal disorders specialist. Because of the merger, the specialists meet and propose forming a partnership with one doing the intestinal disorders, the other the stomach disorders while both keep doing the overlap area that covers many illnesses that can be dealt with on a more or less routine basis.

The chance that both specialists can stay state-of-the-art in their discipline until old obviously increases when the repertoire that each has to keep up with is about half of what it had been before.

Never feel too old to learn from younger masters! The inverted Master-Trainee relationship where older pros learn from younger ones.
Professionals can be distinguished between predominantly Routine work professionals (R pro) and professionals who predominantly work based on Improvisation and Innovation (I pro). All knowledge workers start as I pros and most of them (>80%) develop, via a shorter or longer period as star/high potential, into production tigers and thus become R pros. A smaller group (<20%), however, manages to stay in the star phase until an older age. Those are the I pros with the defining characteristic that they are immune to the half value time of knowledge. These older I pros are ideal teachers for the younger trainees and possibly even for older production tigers: R pros that want to avoid the BS phase by learning from a young master who can help them to refocus their talents. That way, the older R pros again re-enter the trainee phase and start with a new professional life cycle. More about this Master-Trainee relationship later.

First, we will address the inverted Master-Trainee connection, which is a relationship where the master is younger than the trainee. It is similar to children who teach their parents to solve computer problems and how to make the best use of a mobile phone. This is another method to prevent R pros becoming storytellers. Young I pros in the star phase teach state-of-the-art methods and techniques to experienced R pros.

One of the things that the first-line manager (team leader, discipline chairman) can do to avoid sliding off into the BS phase is to tell the older R pro to adhere more strictly to the guidelines, standards and protocols that currently apply to the execution of the profession. Those are never easy discussions. From his start as a trainee, his expertise has kept increasing and he could and was allowed to work with less protocols and guidelines. At the age of 40-45 he was at the zenith of his knowledge, and they called him master and he even renewed the protocols, standards and guidelines. Only 20% or so of the professionals can keep functioning on that master level (the I pros). The others have reached their top and slowly get less knowledgeable mainly where it concerns the information and (new) skill components of their knowledge. That is why in the later phase of their career they have to work by the book again. An often heard reaction from an over-the-hill professional to his manager is: "You have always trusted me and let me do what I wanted and now all of a sudden you start reeling me in. I have always been managed based on output to everybody's satisfaction. I don't understand why you now get involved in my work process and why you check if I stick to the new rules and guidelines. What is the matter with you?" The manager must not be afraid to say that nothing is wrong with him but that instead the professional is simply not as knowledgeable as he used to be, because he is unable to stay up to date in his profession. The older R pro has a wealth of experience; much more than his younger colleague. Also his professional attitude (the approach) will be better, but he never learned those new methods and techniques in his initial education. And even then he never had the time or the inclination to keep learning.

In addition to process-based management, the first-line manager can propose coupling the older R pro to a younger master (star/hipo), but only for the on-the-job, socializing transfer of state-of-the-art methods and techniques.

Knowledge development of the I pro and the R pro and legitimization of the inverted Master-Trainee connection

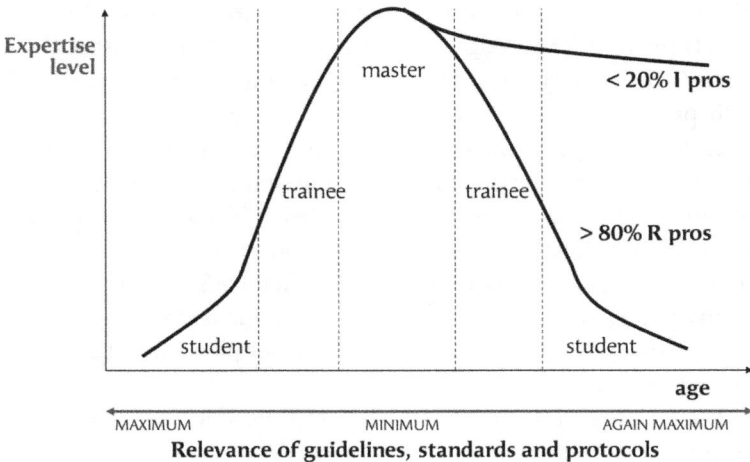

Relevance of guidelines, standards and protocols

A real-life example of an inverted Master-Trainee connection

At a first-rate hospital where I (MW) performed a knowledge management assignment, the chief surgeon felt that it was a pity that some of the older R pros had still not embraced endoscopic operating techniques despite the availability of external training opportunities. I suggested inverted Master-Trainee relationships to enable those older R pros to learn, on the job, from younger surgeons on the team. The reaction from the older gentlemen was predictable. Comments ranged from disqualifying the younger surgeons ("Do you expect me to learn something from these whippersnappers, I thought it was the other way around") to technical disqualification of the method ("In that case we may have to ask the lung tumors to be smaller than 2 inches so that we can extract them between the ribs"). After two months discussion, they finally succeeded in matching the older surgeons to their younger colleagues. The main reason for the final success was the appreciation of the importance of the vast experience of the older surgeons; experience in the approach towards the patient and in essential implicit knowledge more generally known by terms like "clinical insight," "the eye of the master," "the fishy, not-fishy notion."

Never feel too modern to learn from older masters! The traditional Master-Trainee relationship in which the younger knowledge worker learns from the older I pros.

For the sake of clarity, we would like to reiterate the first statement of the previous paragraph: professionals can be distinguished between predominantly Routine work professionals (R pro) and professionals who predominantly work based on Improvisation and Innovation (I pro). All knowledge workers start as I pros and most of them (>80%) develop, via a shorter or longer period as star/high potential, into production tigers and thus become R pros. A smaller group (<20%), however, manages to stay in the star phase until an older age. Those are the I pros with the defining characteristic that they are immune to the half value time of knowledge. These older I pros are ideal teachers for the younger trainees and possibly even for older production tigers: R pros that want to avoid the BS phase by learning from a young master who can help them to refocus their talents. That way the older R pros again re-enter the trainee phase and start with a new professional life cycle.

What we are addressing here is that traditional Master-Trainee relationship.

Together with Margje van de Wiel and Kim Szegedi, psychologists at the University Maastricht, we looked in 2004 at the determining differences in work methods between experienced professionals and masters. The research was held among organization advisors older than 50 and, via peer consultations, it was determined which of them could be considered a master.

The following is a short synopsis of the results of the research:

1) The most important activities for further knowledge development are:
   a) ask for advice from a colleague
   b) evaluate an assignment together
2) Masters do a) and b) more often than experienced professionals
3) Masters spend about twice as much time on (codified) knowledge development than experienced professionals (i.e. reading scientific and trade literature, researching, giving presentations, attending conferences and seminars)
4) Masters "change the plan" more often.

An interesting fact was that masters are less inhibited in asking advice from others (see 2) and that they have less problems with uncertainty (see 4).

When working in a traditional Master-Trainee relationship, it is important to note that older masters in particular do not realize the uniqueness of their knowledge: they are unconsciously talented.

That applies more to I pros that base their mastership more on their experience and artisan skills, like with some architects, oil and gas drilling specialists, surgeons and violinists.

Think of Karel Appel, a famous Dutch painter, who was asked whether he knew why he was a good painter. His answer was: "I just mess around a bit with paint."

In the case of philosophers, physicists and judges, where the state-of-the-art information and analytical skills are relatively important, this state of being unconsciously talented occurs much less. They can usually express in language or signs why they did what they did.

A journalist once asked a famous violinist what the secret was of his success. He briefly thought and said: "My bow handling! I think it has all to do with bow handling. Look." He grabbed the violin and made a few strokes. "That is the way I do it. That is, I think, just a bit different from what most of my colleagues do." The journalist did not know what to do with that information. A masterclass student who had listened to this with a smile spent the next half hour trying to explain to the journalist what her famous teacher probably meant to say.

This example illustrates not only the problem unconscious talented masters usually have explaining their knowledge, it also indicates that the difference in expertise between master and trainee must not be so large that it gets in the way of learning. The knowledge gap between the journalist and the violinist was too large to enable learning. Both the gap between the master and the student and between the student and the journalist were bridgeable.

In master-trainee relationships, learning is only possible if the knowledge gap is not too large

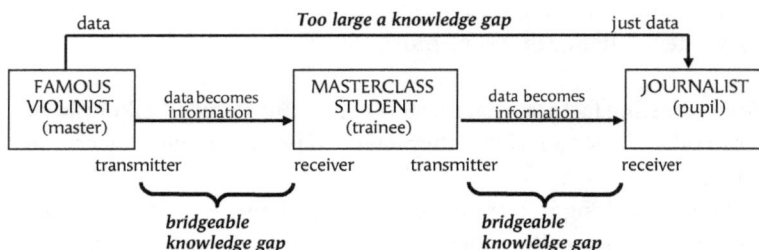

To explain knowledge that you have applied so often that you have become unconsciously gifted, is an art in itself. Try to explain to someone who has never ridden a bicycle how to do it. Knowledge that has become implicit and knowledge that has never been explicit, both of which are locked up in experience and (artisan) skill, must hence be codified, which means: expressed in text, language, or drawings.

The implicit knowledge of the master is usually the source of his ability and many masters are unable or unmotivated to explain that art as a science. Socializing is therefore the most productive way of learning from that category of experienced I pros.

In the middle ages, the guilds played a very important role in the economy. They guarded over the capacity by restricting the number of establishments and masters, and they safeguarded the quality through peer reviews of the master piece that each trainee had to produce after the master had decided that he was ready to do so. This master piece was not only about making the product but also about designing and drawing it. The trainee stayed with his master until another master died or started on his own when the gild decided that expanding the capacity was warranted. Training was by observation and learning by trying.

The organization of an artisanal establishment had the following characteristics:

- A flat structure with many subordinates for each supervisor. This was possible due to the high level of skill of the trainees.
- A strong customer orientation; production was based on the customer's specification, within a certain basic design or standard.
- Knowledge was developed and shared by doing, by collaboration with the master and observing other masters. Occasionally knowledge was written down, as happened in the surgeons guild.
- Problems were solved by experimenting (trial and error).
- Quality control and assurance were linked to personal skills and with the personal honor of the expert.
- Innovation took place:
  a) based on personal creativity, in dialogue between master and customer
  b) by investigating the product of the competition in order to discover improvements and advances and then copying them.
- Later, a distinction was made between design and execution. That breakthrough could be seen in the serial production of ships for the Dutch East India Company and also in the production of paintings (Rembrandt and Vermeer made the initial set-up, trainees worked it out and the master added a finishing touch).

What follows are three real-life examples of the present (traditional) Master-Trainee relationship:

1 The master-advisors

At TCB (The Consultancy Bureau) there was discontent about the effect of the internal training of advisors. The time-to-competence (see Chapter 2) was too long in the sense that it took long for the internal training department to produce clones of the top advisors of the firm. The diagnosis was that the study material was not specific enough for TCB, i.e. did not contribute to the shaping of the particular type of advisor that TCB wanted to see.

In the partner council, three masters were identified – one in each sector – that not only belonged to the top-professionals category, but also had the right attitude. Each master was assigned a younger hipo for one month who would accompany him during his work: in the office, in the car, or on the plane, with the client, etc. The hipo had to document in detail the master's way of working, using my (MW) special templates. During this period, the trainee could ask questions about what the master had said, about what he had (not) seen him doing and about the reason for that. Three reports of 130 pages each would be the final result of the exercise. The reports were then checked and corrected by the master together with the trainee, using terms such as: "I would leave this out, it's not relevant"; "You have left something out here. I see that now that I read it again. At that point I agreed with the client that we ..."; "That is important to mention because in the implementation phase we were able to avoid ..."; "Quite impressive when I read how I do all this."

Currently, the three manuals are the most important input for internal training at TCB and the curricula of the training are renewed in order to capitalize on the explicit knowledge of the TCB masters.

2 The artist at work

At a company where fine mechanical operations are carried out with great precision on precious organic materials, they realized at a certain moment that one of their best people was going to retire in six months' time. Because of that, unique strategically important know-how was going to leave the company. They decided to let Bill carry out a number of complicated operations which would be filmed in detail. Bill was quite flattered by the interest in his work at the end of his career. They made a bunch of slow motion recordings that later were shown frame by frame to those who were meant to take over Bill's work after his retirement. The question was each time: "What does Bill do now and why?"

This gave rise to interesting discussions among the trainees. Sometimes this lead to surprising insights. Trainee 1: "See – he does X again. I don't think this is right, because he leaves too much room for

Y. The instructions say that on no account should you do that at this point!" Trainee 2: "Agreed but look ... You see that? He can now do something that would otherwise not have been possible!" Trainee 3: "Guys, we need to change that in the manual! It is much more efficient that way."

In the second round, the film was shown again frame by frame, but now with the future retiree present. The task was now as follows: "Bill, here are the people who will take over your work and they will now tell you why you do what you're doing." In this way, Bill's artisan skills were made explicit by others and at the same time he could confirm, correct, or add certain interpretations given to his moves: "Now you see this. It looks wrong but it is right for this reason ..."

Thanks to this, Bill's successors have copied his art and his skills are preserved.

3 The masterclass

The problem of a large law firm was that the partners did not have enough time to train the trainees. In those circles, a trainee is a recently graduated lawyer who, if found suitable, can expect an associate position after three years. It is obvious that the chance of that happening is higher if there are internal learning opportunities. And that was exactly the problem. Partners were so busy that there was no time left for them to teach the trainees. It simply took more time to explain things than if they went ahead and solved the problem themselves. On top of that, they did not think much of the quality of the current graduates.

I (MW) advised radically changing the system of trainee allocation. Instead of allocating the new arrivals pro rata to the various sections, small classes of trainees were formed under the supervision of a mentor and, in the first months, these were introduced to all the partners. Following that, each trainee determined which partner he or she would like as a mentor. Since the firm was rather large, this will eventually lead to an allocation which did not deviate that much from the old pro rata system.

Periodically, an internal newsletter was published with the current top 20 of the most elected partners. All this changed the atmosphere in the firm and discussions could be heard in the corridors as: "Good afternoon colleague, did you see, I'm at number 5 in the top 20? I did not notice your name on the list. How come?"

Partners who are in the top 20 realize that they are a role model for young professionals who want to become like them. Training has become a pleasure rather than a burden. On sunny days, you can see the master walking in the park with the trainees explaining what's what. Partners who are not in the top 20 can be exempted from training duties if they so wish.

Culture pessimist Georg Steiner about the destruction of the Master-Trainee relationship:

"Where has the romantic relationship between master and student gone? What has become of the animated transfer of knowledge?"

$$Socrates \Rightarrow Plato \Rightarrow Aristotle$$
$$Jesus \Rightarrow Apostles$$
$$Virgil \Rightarrow Dante$$
$$Abélard \Rightarrow Héloïse$$
$$Husserl \Rightarrow Heidegger \Rightarrow Arendt$$

The new power of the student:
- Progressive pedagogs: More student involvement!
- Education administrators: More passes!
- Students: We know better!
- IT staff, COOs: Google and the computer replace the master!

In Eastern philosophies, the student initially discovers the teacher as the "mouthpiece of reality." The teacher is "the external master," the external guru. As unconditional dedication between the teacher and the student matures, broadens towards complete existence, the student perceives reality as the mouthpiece of the teacher. That is called the discovery of "the internal master" or guru. The classic expression for that is in the land of the spirit, teacher and student are one (de Wit, 1998). That way, the teacher is first example, then spiritual friend, and finally internal master.

In our organizations we prefer "cold learning." That is learning from information which is independent of people: work directives, guidelines, standards, norms, protocols, manuals, drawings, tables, graphs, score cards, etc. "Warm learning" through socializing Master-Trainee relationships happens a lot less and when it happens we consider the experience development as a linear process. We do not see a way back. That is why the introduction of the inverted master is so difficult in practice. That the master should ever want to go back and learn from a student does not fit in our hierarchy-dominated idea of progress. Since the invention of capitalism, continuous growth has been the leading paradigm. Tomorrow we must have more than today. Standing still means going backwards, hesitation means weakness, and he who thinks that after many years he can still learn something from a novice is naive and loses power. Many of our "masters" are primarily focused on further egocentric development; they are continuously motivated to improve the skills that are necessary to reach a higher position or at least to be able to successfully defend the position they have already achieved. But a master without students is invisible and therefore not a master.

> "Every teacher is a student of his teacher and the highest teacher ends up as the student of a novice. That is why in Japanese martial arts the white belt is the highest as well as the lowest level." (Vernooy, 2000)

Away with the life phase conscious HR management!
The new fad in HRM is called life phase personnel management which is no good at all. It's not at all good because it takes the premise that going through the sequence trainee-star-production tiger-storyteller correlates with increased age. In the old days, when the half value time of knowledge was not as short as it is now, that did apply. But now, professionals pass through such a sequence (if they don't become managers) twice or three times, especially in knowledge-intensive organizations that work with T-profiles and (inverted) Master-Trainee relationships. Put another way: at modern knowledge-intensive organizations there are trainees who are 22, 33 and 44 years old.

More opportunities to learn
The title of this chapter is: offer professionals continuous opportunities to learn so that they can remain involved in their profession with state-of-the-art knowledge.

In addition to T profiles and inverted Master-Trainee relationships, there are more ways of avoiding becoming a storyteller:

Characteristics of the group culture of trainees, stars, production tigers and storytellers

high	STARS/HIPOS:	TRAINEES:
	- are individualistic and assertive - are ambitious and competitive (win – lose; "See you on the BoD") - think that everything can and must be done differently - have little regard for work/life balance	- are focused on the Great Experts in the organization (not the hierarchy) - are insecure; want to know which way they are judged, want feedback - want to belong - have a strong team spirit
	PRODUCTION TIGERS:	STORYTELLERS:
low	- are good in working together (win – win) - pay more attention to quality than to innovation - are self-managing - are faithful to the organization and loyal to the hierarchy	- are interested in outside activities - idealize "the old days" - look for social contact (commiseration) during work - are often isolated; "internal dismissal"

Left axis: Expected growth in performance (high to low)

Bottom axis: **high**　　　**Relevance of the present performance**　　　**low**

- Take a sabbatical of six to twelve months: step back from day-to-day business and reflect on redirecting your talents. Answer questions such as: what do I want, what can I do, and what may I do? Make a plan for your professional future based on the answers, discuss that plan with friends and start studying again. A sabbatical is particularly suitable after you have spent a few years as a group or team leader and want to return (full-time) to your profession. In the latter case the sabbatical is taken at the moment when you pass the baton to the group member who is next in line. You have probably strayed from your discipline in those years of leading and managing. In which case it would be really good to take your time to bring your knowledge up to scratch and to make a solid decision about which direction you want to pursue in your future career before returning to the workplace.
- Spend a few years dedicating one or two days a week to reflecting on the experiences gained over the past years by writing a book or doing a so-called executive PhD. Re-immerse yourself in academia to emerge after a while invigorated with renewed knowledge.
- Teach for some time at a college or school (part-time). That is a

particularly good strategy if you have lost touch with whatever you really liked about your discipline.
- Start working part-time e.g. go from 100% to 60% and spend the rest of the time at another organization to get new ideas; to experience other ways of working; to facilitate your own out-of-the-box thinking; etc.
- All sorts of combinations of the abovementioned possibilities.

Management can add to that a number of less drastic possibilities to stimulate learning:
- introducing Personal Commitment Statements with learning targets (see also Chapter 4)
- making self-assessment instruments available
- periodically determining of the present and desired level of knowledge per employee (competency management)
- *éducation permanente*: offering internal and external training courses and attending conferences and exhibitions
- organizing peer group reviews
- organizing project evaluation meetings
- applying job rotation (carrousels) and temporary part-time internal postings

In the title of this chapter, we mentioned a relationship between learning and involvement. What follows now illustrates such a relationship.

At a conference in Geneva, one of the speakers was a high-ranking manager of the Gartner Group and he presented the following thesis: "I'd rather invest in training people who might leave, than not invest in people who might stay. Of course there are people that leave because they want to capitalize on their state-of-the-art knowledge with the competition; people that want to profit from the many opportunities that Gartner provides for people to learn. But most of our people stay, because they know that they can remain good at their profession until the end of their career. Also, I do not want to stay awake at night thinking that people stay with us because no one else wants them. I want them to be so good that only one telephone call is needed for them to get another job, but that they don't do that because they like working with us. There is a family feeling, sense of belonging, team spirit, and we have a collective ambition based on many shared values."

So it really is simple: if you want your people to be involved, you must invest heavily in creating learning opportunities. And by doing that you indicate to them that you consider it important that professionals stay. The other side of the coin is what could be called "intensive people farming": you do not invest in people but use them until their knowledge is obsolete and then kick them out. They use great words like contract management, knowledge valorization and employability. But it is simple Anglo-American opportunism: take the knowledge and run!

When the wise lessons from this chapter are applied, chances are that in the knowledge workplace, the percentage of professionals that is involved and has state-of-the-art expertise will increase dramatically.

Such an involved professional is somebody who:
- continues to have access to state-of-the-art knowledge, and has learned to learn fast
- furthers the discipline, innovates
- feels and takes responsibility for his own tasks (PCS) and for the collective ambition of the organization, which as a result works better together
- shares his knowledge with others inside and outside the organization, driven by involvement with the organization and with the environment in which they operate
- shows that he loves his work.

Making T profiles together

1a First fill out Form A with the T profile that you want to have in the future:
- that may be the same as your current profile (current situation = desired situation)
- the T profile is related to the professional knowledge and skills (it is not about qualities in leadership, management, market approach, etc.)

1b Visualize your T on Form A; for help and inspiration see the examples of T profiles

2 Find two colleagues and form a group of three people. Divide the time left by three and go through the following procedure three times:
- A explains his or her T profile to B and C
- B and C ask A critical questions and give constructive feedback

3 Adjust your T profile based on the received feedback and note the corrected T profile on Form B to be handed in

4 Indicate on the basis of the corrected T profile (also on Form B) the learning effort (education, training, learning on the job, Master-Trainee relationship, etc.) that you want to make to realize or retain your future desired T profile.

Examples of T profiles to help with question 1b.

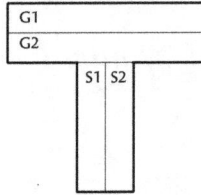

Standard T

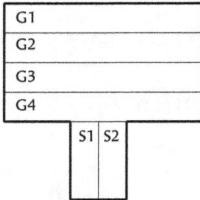

4 generalisms
2 (shallow) specializations

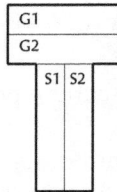

2 narrower generalisms
2 specializations

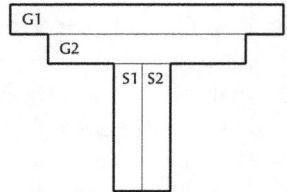

1 broad generalism
1 generalism
2 specializations

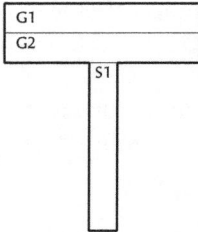

2 generalisms
1 super specializations

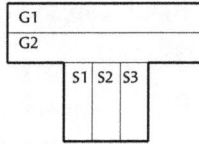

2 generalisms
3 (shallow) specializations

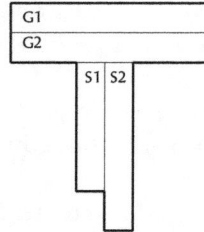

2 generalisms
1 specialization
1 super specialization

... and all possible variations and combinations

FORM A

Desired future T profile of:

GENERALISMS:
(name the 4 [maximum] most important subjects, disciplines, knowledge areas, that you want to master on a generalist level)

G1: ————————————————————————————————
————————————————————————————————

G2: ————————————————————————————————
————————————————————————————————

G3: ————————————————————————————————
————————————————————————————————

G4: ————————————————————————————————
————————————————————————————————

SPECIALISMS:
(name the 2 [maximum] most important professional methods, professional techniques that you want to master on a specialist level)

S1: ————————————————————————————————
————————————————————————————————

S2: ————————————————————————————————
————————————————————————————————

Visualization of my T profile:

MY T PROFILE, adjusted version

FORM B

Desired future T profile of:

GENERALISMS:
(name the 4 [maximum] most important subjects, disciplines, knowledge areas, working methods that you want to master on a generalist level)

G1: ———————————————————————————
—————————————————————————————
—————————————————————————————

G2: ———————————————————————————
—————————————————————————————
—————————————————————————————

G3: ———————————————————————————
—————————————————————————————
—————————————————————————————

G4: ———————————————————————————
—————————————————————————————
—————————————————————————————

SPECIALISMS:
(name the 2 [maximum] most important professional methods, professional techniques that you want to master on a specialist level)

S1: ————————————————————————————
—————————————————————————————
—————————————————————————————

S2: ————————————————————————————
—————————————————————————————
—————————————————————————————

Visualization of my T profile:

In future I want to learn more about:

6 MANAGEMENT STYLE

Inspire professionals, BE there, dare to differentiate, function as heat shield against "noise from above" and love their work.

In this chapter we will address the six most important tasks for someone who leads a group of professionals.

Task # 1: The shared development of a collective ambition
If someone held a gun to my head and I had to make a choice, then this is the most important task for a manager of a group of professionals: the creation of the process to explicate in violent interaction with each other the collective ambition of the group and the self-involvement in that process, to the extent that the manger gives the kick-off by stating the values that he personally has experienced and observed. Then comes the demonstration of the collective ambition, continuously keeping it alive through context-dependent interpretation and bi-annual updating.

What a collective ambition is and why it is necessary is fully explained in Chapter 1 and its addendum. Two examples there explain how to arrive at such a collective ambition. Here, we will further address the consequences of investing in a collective ambition, something that is often qualified by Anglo-American opponents as soft talk about shared values and raison d'être as a negative side effect. By explicating the shared values that give direction to the desired way of working and interaction, a category of professionals can be identified that: achieve good professional or financial results, but arrive at those results in a way that does not fit the shared values of the organization. And if you do not have shared values based on collective ambition, then you simply can't "see" the line A-B in the next matrix. Our conviction, based on extensive real-life experience, is that the advantage of having a collective ambition far outweighs the disadvantage of becoming aware of this group of "brilliant misfits." Also the undesirable side effect lessens with the realization that such a group of brilliant non-conformists *exists* and when you wonder as a manager how to deal with these professionals.

The following argument aims to help you in this. It is based on a matrix that was presented by Jack Welch, former CEO of General Electric at a conference. The most important modification to this matrix that we allowed ourselves to make is the replacement of the word "manager" with "professional." That is justified because Jack Welch was unchallenged in his days, and because (like Iacocca at Chrysler) he had no direct working relationship with the professionals in the workplace at GE; he was the manager managing those managers.

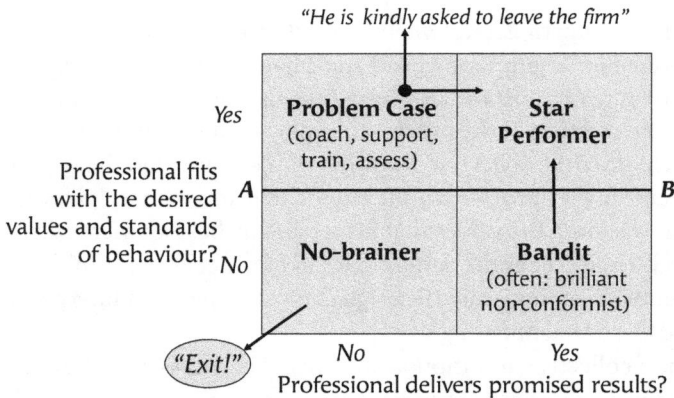

A-B: Jack Welch: "*It takes several years to know who is above or below the line*"

You can, without any problem, keep managing the Star Performer on output: he achieves the targets agreed in the PCS and also does that in a way that matches the organization's desired style of working. The Problem Case also does the latter but does not achieve the agreed results, so he gets coaching, support and training and is re-assessed after some time. If he has then reached the agreed targets, he enters the class of Star Performers. Is he unsuccessful, then nothing can be done further and he is – like Jack says – "Kindly asked to leave the premises." Then there is the professional that Jack calls in no uncertain terms the "No-brainer." That is someone that does not reach the targets and does that in a way that does not fit the shared values of the organization. Away with that man! Out!

And then finally that difficult category of Bandits, productive anarchists, disobedient winners, eccentric prima donnas. How to handle them? That question is easier put than answered. Often these folks do not only get to their targets but they surpass them big time, which makes it even more difficult to "reel them in" appropriately. They want to work in funny places and at funny times. I (MW) know an Australian surgeon who has been living in Europe for some time now and still lives on Australian time. He prefers to do his most difficult operations at 3 am, which drives the anesthetist and the OR personnel crazy and leaves the family wondering in despair: "Why is our Charles being operated now? Is the doctor still fit enough?" These prima donnas allow themselves all sorts of privileges: a top-level consultant that keeps writing his reports with a pen and who has this typed out by a secretary because he cannot think in front of a screen ("Then you simply get bad advice. I can't concentrate the same way with a mouse as I can with pen and paper"); a brilliant researcher that wants a pinball machine in his lab because if he gets stuck he finds a way out by playing the machine; a brilliant tax advisor who neglects his personal hygiene (unshaven, unpolished shoes, wrinkled shirt, etc.); a great criminal law attorney who can only write his celebrated pleadings if he is assisted by a "nice looking" female trainee ("Somehow I get stimulated"); a successful scientist who does not want to move to the new building and instead wants to write his publications from his garden shed ("My productivity slows down dramatically if I have to sit in an office building. I can sense it"); a top musician who is sure that he is going to give a bad concert if he does not have a changing room with ... see list. Way back in 1939, the then very young professor Horowitz was sent home by Philips himself to "mess around" further with what would shortly become the world famous Philishave electric razor. All examples of professionals who surpass their targets but do so in a way that does not fit in with the shared values of an organization. Lots of similar particularities can be mentioned about famous scientists such as Einstein with his uncombed appearance and Niels Bohr with his pipe, etc., all eccentrics in their own right. Krupp had his office above the stables at his villa Huegel in Essen, Germany, because he could not work without the "stimulating" smell of horse dung below. Luckily for him there were no cars around in those days. They needed to set themselves apart from the mainstream to generate their original ideas without being hampered by conventions and prejudices, and thus make those giant scientific steps forward or create new technologies. It is a mindset.

The world needs these people so how can we keep them?

- Quantitative or qualitative "lowering" of the line A-B. It means: define fewer shared values or underplay the importance of (some of) these values. Eventually, there will be fewer professionals that can be accused of eccentric behavior.

- Raising the targets for the brilliant non-conformists. They derive their right to work in a non-conformist way to a large extent from the fact that they are so good at their profession and that they also quantitatively reach their targets. More often than not, they surpass their targets by a factor of two or three. Raising the targets for a Bandit increases the chance that he will not surpass the target by too large a margin, which in turn weakens his feeling that a number of values and standards do not apply to him. But be careful, because he may get frustrated and lose interest.

- Simply accept that brilliant non-conformists exist. Talk down criticism of their behavior by pointing out the advantages of these obstinate prima donnas. In a quantitative sense, their numbers must be kept restricted (1 in 20?) because otherwise the line A-B becomes implausible; shared values by definition only exist by the grace of a more or less uniformly thinking majority. Should there be a particular professional that makes objections against the acceptance of such a productive anarchist, then the manager can, if necessary, impose the following Machiavellian decision rule: "If you are as good as him you may do the same." In fact, what you tell him is that if you are very good you can buy more freedom. Not nice, but effective.

WARNING! Always be aware of the fact that these brilliant non-conformists often need to demonstrate their eccentricity by isolating themselves from others. Lowering their "profile" can frustrate them and may undermine their creativity.

Not all managers are motivated to invest time and energy in the development of a collective ambition. Some do not see the need, others are too busy with themselves or are too sciences-oriented to appreciate the philosophy behind it. The following classification of managers sheds some more light on this, which in turn leads to the following recommendations:

- cherish the manager who finds continuity more important than profit and who values his profesision more than power and money. (In Continental Europe, this type of manager is also called a Rhineland manager)
- send the Planning & Control Technocrat back to the cookie factory and
- overload the Egocentric Manager with so many tasks that are too difficult for him that he eventually leaves.

The **Rhineland manager** knows that investing in a collective ambition and the continuing supply of learning opportunities and professional challenges is essential in binding and captivating professionals. That is why he likes employees with a T profile (see Chapter 5), stimulates multidisciplinary collaboration and job rotation and is always looking for cross-functional and inter-departmental synergies. He sees several part-time jobs for the same employee in various sections of the organization as the ideal way to eliminate tunnel vision. His preferred style is output review of self-managing professionals or teams based on previously agreed, challenging but attainable personal or team commitment statements (PCS, TCS see Chapter 4).

He will try to avoid:

- a coasting routine attitude of professionals repeating things that they have done before and are already good at
- gaining short-term efficiency at the expense of innovation and the development and long-term effectiveness of the professional.

The Rhineland manager creates a learning organization through continuously offering opportunities to learn and to learn how to learn. He is a master in discovering and deploying the unique competencies of people. IT is mainly used to find synergy and the right people to work with face-to-face.

The **P&C (planning & control) Technocrat** uses IT mainly to plan and check the work of the employees in a bureaucratic way. He lives in his management cockpit and feels like Major Tom when he touches his controls on the dashboard. He does not mind employees working from home, employees on temporary contracts, external advisors, external scientists, and the like. Loyalty, commitment, family feeling, shared values, and a sense of belonging are romantic terms that he does not rate highly. Sessions "out in the country" where collective ambitions and mission statements are developed are something he finds, at best, good for the informal contacts but more often than not a waste of time. Bonding and captivating are non-issues. It is all about business and contract management. The advances of information technology help him plan these contracts and monitor and control them.

The P&C Technocrat thinks that offering learning opportunities is not his task. Professionals are themselves responsible for furthering their expertise. Employability schemes enable employees to get a personal budget to maintain their market value by buying education and training. Collectively protected work relations are therefore superfluous. The world has become an infinite Global Casino and virtual and real networks take care of the rest.

The **Egocentric Manager** is a power-driven leader who is only interested in his own career. All he can think of is "how to get to the top." Employees, colleagues, and higher managers are pawns, allies, or rivals and if they do not fit into any of these categories, they can best be ignored. His motto is: don't ask what you can do for the company, but ask what the company can do for you. If the creation of a collective ambition or offering learning opportunities to employees gives him a good press, he will do it because that will further his own ambitions. The Egocentric Manager deploys IT mainly to gain knowledge about the people who play an important role in certain situations. In addition, he can efficiently influence the changing networks and coalitions, often by making slick use of the CC function in emails. His enthusiasm for his profession or for the knowledge domain of the section that he leads is related to the influence that enthusiasm has on his career development. He is more a politician than a manager.

Task # 2: Inspiring people
In the 1980s, when Lee Iacocca used his quarterly review system at
Chrysler, he noted that the system had two potential problems. "First,
people sometimes would bite off more than they can chew. But any su-
pervisor worth his salt would much rather deal with people who attempt
too much than those who try too little. The other problem is the boss'
tendency to interfere too early. You have to resist this temptation. The
quarterly review is self-regulating: it works best if you don't interfere.
Most managers are reluctant to let their people run with the ball, but
you'd be surprised how fast an informed and motivated guy can run."

25 years ago Lee already knew that inspired professionals – even without a collective ambition – become self-managing. Add a common
goal and they also become self-organizing.

A manager who can inspire the people who have been entrusted to
him in such a way that – like him – they believe that their collective
ambition is not pie in the sky, can relax. "Do not organize and there is
organization." Lao-tse said it long ago: "The Sage manages his affairs
without ado and yet nothing is left undone." That is why we say:
"Managing professionals? Don't!", and that is quite different from
"do nothing!" Because he observes well, a wise leader does what needs
to be done and no more. A lot of busy management is a sign of insecurity and stupefaction. Acting without being awake only leads to chaos
and slogans.

So what about motivation? Don't they need to be motivated? No!
Professionals have studied to work. They have invested many years in
their study so that they are positioned to indulge themselves even
longer in their chosen profession. Professionals are therefore intrinsically motivated. What a shame then that many professionals find it
difficult to remain motivated, due to MBAs and other process managers who have no roots in the profession that is practiced in the
workplace. "If you push someone in the direction he is moving toward, will he go faster? No, he will automatically resist!" Many professionals who experience that are intrinsically motivated *until* the
boss comes in. That is why bosses must first and foremost inspire
(stir, arouse) and when it comes to motivation (enthuse, stimulate)
do less of it rather than more. Enjoying the professional results that
have been achieved together, whereby the first-line manager is seen

as one of the team members, is so much more pleasant than a work situation that is typified as "we do a good job but that is in spite of management, rather than thanks to management."

Compared with Welch's theory how does this sound?
The most fulfilling thing for me as a manager is to watch someone the system has labeled as just average or mediocre really come into his own, all because someone has listened to his problems and helped him solve them.
Management is nothing more than motivating other people. Or: the more Dave feels he has set his own goals, the more likely it is that he'll go right through a brick wall in order to reach them.

Lee Iacocca

Planning & control versus self-management:
What do you want the organization to look like?

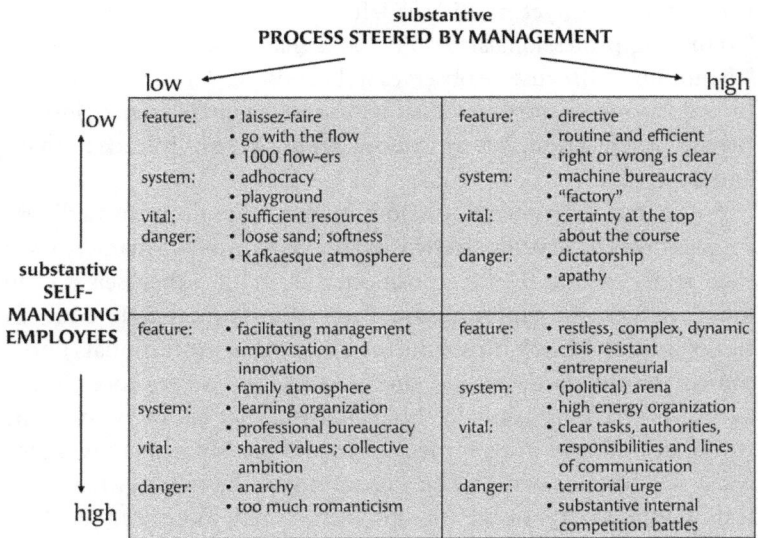

substantive
PROCESS STEERED BY MANAGEMENT

low ←————————→ high

low ↑	feature:	• laissez-faire • go with the flow • 1000 flow-ers	feature:	• directive • routine and efficient • right or wrong is clear
	system:	• adhocracy • playground	system:	• machine bureaucracy • "factory"
	vital: danger:	• sufficient resources • loose sand; softness • Kafkaesque atmosphere	vital: danger:	• certainty at the top about the course • dictatorship • apathy
substantive **SELF-** **MANAGING** **EMPLOYEES**	feature:	• facilitating management • improvisation and innovation • family atmosphere	feature: system:	• restless, complex, dynamic • crisis resistant • entrepreneurial • (political) arena • high energy organization

	system:
	vital:
		• learning organization
		• professional bureaucracy
		• shared values; collective
		  ambition
			vital:	• clear tasks, authorities,
				  responsibilities and lines
				  of communication

↓ **high**	danger:	• anarchy • too much romanticism	danger:	• territorial urge • substantive internal competition battles

Assuming there is a collective ambition and that the people are good at their profession, one can rely on the intrinsic motivation of self-managing and self-organizing professionals who will realize that ambition.

Self-organizing means that the manager can dispense with all sorts of motivating, rules, procedures and job descriptions which he formally used to control the work of the professionals. Instead, the first-line manager inspires the professional and clearly and continuously, by whatever means, communicates the collective ambition and the goals derived from it. If the manager does that well and sincerely, if he radiates trust in "his" people and if the goals are challenging yet attainable, the professionals themselves will allocate and coordinate the work in order to reach the objectives. A real-life example* that beautifully illustrates the differences between self-management and *management by planning & control* is in traffic. Depending on the number of cars that are at a crossing, the planning & control perspective gets more regulated. It goes from: left yields, then to traffic lights, followed by street markings. What is clear is that there are two things people who meet each other at crossings do NOT have to do: think and cooperate. Everything in that respect is taken care of with lines and colored lights (an excellent solution for an environment where you find predominantly *dumb and anti-social people or people that do not enjoy thinking)*. The alternative is a roundabout or a 4-way junction in the US. It is self-organizing. If they are to achieve a common goal (to continue their way) at such a roundabout, people must think and cooperate with fellow traffic participants. You could say that at such intersections you see the coming and going of short lived self-managing teams.

Of course, self-management and self-organization are skills that do not just happen. They require gradual development.

* Ton van Asseldonk (TVA Developments, Veldhoven) at a BIS conference in the Netherlands.

Phases in the development of a self-managing team

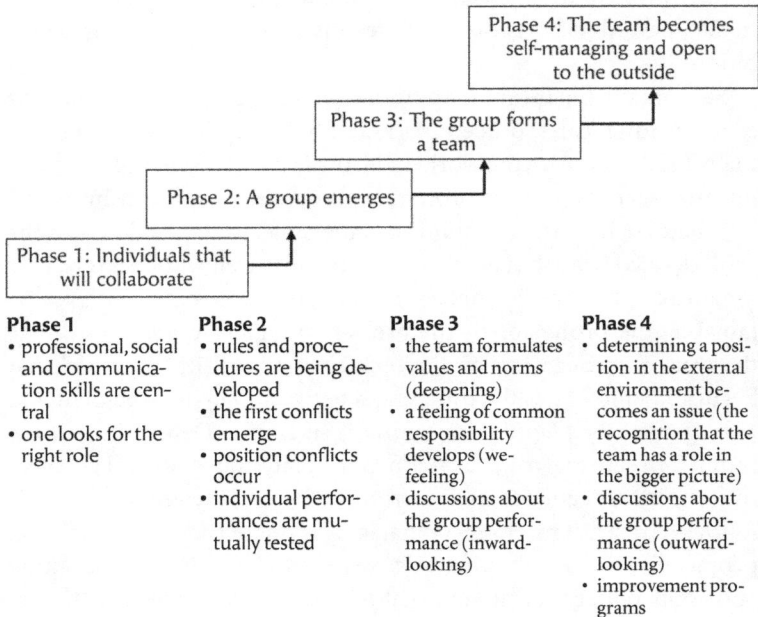

```
                                        ┌────────────────────────┐
                                        │ Phase 4: The team becomes│
                                        │ self-managing and open  │
                                        │        to the outside   │
                                        └────────────────────────┘
                           ┌──────────────────────────┐
                           │ Phase 3: The group forms  │
                           │          a team           │
                           └──────────────────────────┘
                  ┌──────────────────────────┐
                  │ Phase 2: A group emerges  │
                  └──────────────────────────┘
       ┌──────────────────────────┐
       │ Phase 1: Individuals that │
       │     will collaborate      │
       └──────────────────────────┘
```

Phase 1	Phase 2	Phase 3	Phase 4
• professional, social and communication skills are central • one looks for the right role	• rules and procedures are being developed • the first conflicts emerge • position conflicts occur • individual performances are mutually tested	• the team formulates values and norms (deepening) • a feeling of common responsibility develops (we-feeling) • discussions about the group performance (inward-looking)	• determining a position in the external environment becomes an issue (the recognition that the team has a role in the bigger picture) • discussions about the group performance (outward-looking) • improvement programs

(Van Amelsfoort and Scholtes, 1997)

Task # 3: Be there, observe well and really communicate

The Avatamsaka Sutra teaches us that there is only "inter-being," that nothing exists separately and independently, and that nothing has an identity in itself.

Without "you" there is no "I," without "that" there is no "this." No one, nothing exists alone.

The organization is a playground for inter-being; the playing field on which a collective reaches the goal that has been reached. The energy of the collective is that of everyone. Without a collective, nobody is visible. And without somebody no collective can exist.

"None of us is as good as all of us," is an enlightened slogan of McDonalds.

It was the second week of January and I (MW) was invited by the specialists of the cardiology section to a large hospital's New Year's reception. The year before, I had satisfactorily completed an advisory task and hence I was invited. I stood there with a glass in my hand with a small group of cardiologists and listened to the New Year's speech. Then I overheard one of the specialists asking a colleague: "Who is that guy?" "That is Mr. So-and-so our group manager," was the answer. "Oh is that our group manager. Sorry, but you know I have only been here for three months."

See, that is someone who works somewhere for three months and in all that time he has not met his boss. Such a boss is actually not there. How can you inspire people? How can you communicate meaningfully? You cannot!

Ideal managers of professionals live and work among the workers who have been entrusted to them. They do not conglomerate in a management corridor on the top floor of a prestigious over-designed HQ, but have a room that is physically near the laboratories, workshops and offices of the professionals. The farther the manager is from the workplace, the more formal communication with the workers becomes, the bigger the difference between trade jargon and the MBA language from "above," the more managers rely on IT and paper realities and the more difficult it is to really care. Unknown = unloved.

"We can't even get past the air hostesses"

When asked to advise somewhere, I (MW) always send out a letter first with a short explanation of my way of working. One of the most important conditions is that I get a chance for at least half a day to get to know the people in the workplace. The value of an organization is always determined by the products they make in the workplace. What are the people doing who make these products day in and day out and what is the beauty in doing that? If you dispense with that, every organization will look the same. You only see the parking lot for the visitors, the lift or the escalator to the top floor and the glasshouse management wing stuffed with art.

I was asked to look into improving vertical communication. The management of the high-tech company with more than 1,500 employees discovered during a retreat session that they were too "Olympically" positioned and were disconnected from the workplace. I mentioned that to one of the engineers in the workplace. "Good point," he said, "we can't even get past the air hostesses." Before I could ask for an explanation, I was called away by a secretary who accompanied me via the escalators up to the management quarters. There I was welcomed by two uniformed ladies. Aha, these are the "air hostesses" I thought. The secretary handed me over to them and one of them said: "You are Mr. Weggeman I presume, and you are here to see Mr. van der Berg? The CEO has just walked into Mr. van der Berg's office and as you may understand we cannot ask the CEO to go away just because Mr. Weggeman is here, which is why Mr. van der Berg kindly asks you to wait for a few minutes if you don't mind. Can I offer you a cup of coffee?" After about 15 minutes the other "air hostess" appeared. "Mr. Weggeman, we are very sorry about all this but now Mr. van der Berg has to take an unexpected phone call from an important acquaintance from China. You may use one of our internet workstations so you can check your email." Finally, after 25 minutes I passed a designer coat rack which I did not dare to use because I thought it was some sort of statue, left two designer secretaries behind and ended up in Mr. van der Berg's ballroom office. "How good of you to come, Mr. Weggeman, see our problem is that we feel disconnected from the workplace." "You don't say!" I thought, and that's how my survey started. After a number of interviews, a bit of desk research and participating observation, my advice was to decentralize the managers. Physically. Instead of them staying together in their glass palace, I proposed that each of them relocate to the building where most of his or her people worked. Not on the top floor, not on the bottom floor but right smack in the middle. As far as possible surrounded by the professionals. Protests galore: "Bad advice," "Do you think that we would not have thought of this ourselves if it was such a good idea?" ("No.") "The offices there are too small. We are used to large offices with six windows; there the largest offices only have four." I told them that you can adjust all that, for them to try it for a few months and that we would then evaluate things and if it did not work we could always turn things around. Reluctantly they agreed. After two months, as was agreed, I made an evaluation and went around all the new decentralized offices of the managers. In one of the offices I even saw a white coat hanging on a no-nonsense cloak hanger. "Hi John," I said "have you found your old lab coat again?" "Yes," he smiled, "it's fun. When an experiment has come to a critical phase, they call me to come and have a look. Last week, I got such a call from one of the boys who said: 'John, it is about to happen: we have to see a blue light within half an hour, or we won't see it again for another six months.' So I go there. They like it and so do I. It is nice to see what you are actually managing."

The upshot of it all was that all the managers thought the experiment was a success and they had decided unanimously to stay in their new "smaller" offices. Their former glasshouse management wing was transformed into a meeting centre – the rooms were big enough – and the entry hall had been turned into a sort of restaurant with the "air hostesses" behind the bar. The management team starts each morning with a coordination breakfast meeting in the restaurant and then each goes to "their" respective buildings. Within six months, vertical communication had markedly improved, and the professionals as well as the managers clearly felt that they were there for each other, that there was more time and increased attention.

The Boss is too far from the battle front

Martijn Lovers claims that in business we can learn a lot from war history and in particular from the German way of fighting: "First the generals set a goal and then they leave it to the troops to develop the best way to achieve it. All the soldiers know the objective. When the general dies, the fight can continue because the level under him knows the strategic goal and is well trained. In the Anglo-Saxon world, hierarchy and procedures are more important. The CEO is the boss and often stays in an ivory tower far away from the frontline. If he does not know how to proceed, nobody will." When working for the international publisher Reed Elsevier, he saw how the Anglo-Saxon "top-down" mentality destroyed all traces of creativity. Everyone was defending his own position. Each month, a ranking was made of the twenty business units based on paper calculations. If you were in one of the worst three units you had to report to the manager. Some turned stealing turnover into a game. Not surprisingly, the banking crisis started in the United States. "No one reports to the top about the risks that were taken."

Be there and really and timely communicate

Personal management for us means:
- Be honest; don't play games
- Grant others the honor; don't flaunt other people's achievements
- Don't let your people down to the outside (also don't "over-sell")
- Immediately address even the smallest issues
- Don't just be easily accessible and contactable, but be proactive and go to the employees in their workplace
- Give people clear signals, but do not hurt them
- Challenge the professionals; ask provoking questions
- Know about contentions, make them legitimate, discuss them, respect them
- Allow rivalry but only within the application of the group's mission.
From a presentation in 1990 by Dr Anton van Veijfeiken, manager of the Innovation Management Consultancy group of Philips Electronics

From an Oriental Angle The Buddha preached three ways of acquiring insight: observe, reflect and meditate; all three are linked and every single one cannot exist without the two others. Observing is listening to what the situation tells you; focused, without distraction, barriers, obstructions, or prejudice.

Reflecting or contemplating is reflecting on what has been observed; it is exploring the consequences.

Meditating is the embodiment of newly acquired insights; it is the manifestation of what has been observed and reflected upon; it is making sense of what has been seen.

Really seeing and listening, really reflecting and really being who you are requires courage:

• Do you have the courage to observe more and analyze less?
• Do you have the courage to reflect more and judge less?
• Do you have the courage to meditate more and have fewer meetings?

Satisfaction, at home and at work, develops in a continuing circle of uninhibited get-togethers and being consciously present. "The less we see our fellow humans through a filter of our own self-interest, the more this enables real engagement characterized by compassion. Then we are not only able to feel joy at someone's prosperity, but are also able and willing to see the suffering of others." (De Wit, 1998).

For those who are driven by self-interest, the world can be used (and even abused) to further oneself. That urge often goes hand in hand with a lack of empathy and patience. Such an attitude frustrates a fruitful development of openness to meet people and promote attentive presence. As a result, the dissatisfaction in our organizations will endure.

Often, we too quickly ask the question: "What shall we do, which actions are we going execute?" We want to do so much that there is no time to ask those four key questions that should precede the what-to-dos: "What have we seen?", "What do we see here now?", "What have we learned?" and "What are we learning here now?" We consider it dangerous to postpone action while we first answer those questions, because a lot of things could happen while we wait.

Be in the here and now

"When I sit, I sit. When I stand, I stand. When I go, I go," said the man. "But that is also what I do," the other man interrupted. "No," replied the first, "When you sit, you already stand. When you stand, you already walk. And when you walk, you are already there."
(Arabic proverb).

Task # 4: Dare to differentiate (= manage based on output unless ...)
Managers must dare to differentiate and professionals have the right to be differentiated, because in the workplace at knowledge-intensive organizations there is no equality. Only there, where people cannot make a difference (as in the cookie factory) you cannot differentiate in management style. However, if people can make a difference, then there *must* be differentiation. It is like we said in Chapter 4, repeating this here is far from superfluous, because this is the core of managing professionals and particularly because, in practice, it rarely happens.

Professionals that *have* achieved their PCS need to be managed differently from professionals who haven't. Routine type workers (R pros) must be handled differently from dominating innovating professionals (I pros). Trainees are different from star/hipos who in turn must be managed differently from production tigers, who again have to be treated differently from the storytellers.*

The necessary differentiation in management style toward professionals that achieve their PCS (output-based management) and professionals who cannot do that (throughput-based management) is addressed in Chapter 4. What follows is a reproduction of the desired management care and style for trainees, star/hipos, production tigers, and storytellers; whereby it is good to know that I pros are often stars/hipos and R pros, production tigers.

Trainees must be given the feeling that you trust them, that they are talented and able, (otherwise you would not have hired them), but that their talents have to be directed toward the collective ambition of the organization. Trainees need clear tasks ("On what will I be assessed?") and lots of real-time and clear feedback because they want to learn. That is particularly true for young trainees, the "screenagers" that enter our organizations. Trainees must be made familiar with the organizational culture, with the unwritten rules, answers to questions like: how do you celebrate your birthday here, if at all? Is it generally the case that when you make an appointment, it is always scheduled in the office of the highest ranking colleague? Can you discuss mistakes you made or is it better not to?

---

* See Chapter 4 for PCS and Chapter 5 for the trainee/star-hipo/production tiger/storyteller classification.

Certainly at large organizations it is useful to have a trainee follow short training sessions of 4-6 weeks to get to know the departments that he will not or only seldom have dealings with during the first phase of his career. An example: someone has been taken on for the engineering department, follows short sessions at the marketing and corporate finance department, and someone that has got a job as a brand manager does that in R&D and logistics.

Stimulate assertiveness in trainees. Ask them what they think is strange, funny, illogical or incorrect. I (MW) know an engineering agency where every trainee after 100 days has to write a report entitled: "Observations of a newcomer." After 100 days, the well-known company blindness rapidly sets in. At that agency, these reports are the main source for organizational and process innovation.

If there is one category likely to become overworked then it is the **star/high potentials** group. Because they are generally not troubled by low success fantasies they tend to take on more and more tasks:

- either because of territorial instinct, thinking that a particular task is part of their area of responsibility: "This is typically an advanced development project so that belongs here and I am going to take charge of it. I simply do not understand why research wants this, have they got nothing else to do?"
- or because they think that is also a nice task: "It's a challenge!"
- or because they simply consider the other guy not good enough to do it: "We must not mess up this great opportunity by giving it to Roger. Then it will all come to nothing. Better give it to me."

You can keep up such a high-energy and high-commitment attitude for some time but at a given moment you collapse. The solution is for the first-line manager to curtail drastically the number of projects and innovations allocated to such an individual. There are limits, even for a hipo. In the same vein, it is advisable to dim the often self-centeredness and arrogance of the star by forcing him to show respect towards his lesser talented colleagues. A basketball team with only Shaquille O'Neals or a soccer team with only Pelés and Cruijffs would not get far as a team.

Furthermore, there is no other category of professionals where you have to address the balance between work and family life in their staff report. At a management seminar with first-line managers of clinical departments of hospitals, there was a discussion about whether something was a matter for a department head to deal with or not. The example was set at the internal medicine department of a large well-known hospital. Spending a number of years working as a nurse used to be seen as good preparation for motherhood. That is still the case, but upgrading has also struck here and nowadays a few years training as an intern is seen as even better. Young female interns apply for a job and immediately say that they only want to do that for a few years because then they want to have a child. Then the job turns out to be so demanding, they feel so needed and involved and they are so enthusiastic about the work that they put off having children for another year and then for another year and so on. The question was whether the department head had to bring up this change of pattern sooner rather than later. The vote was a draw. One group did not think so. The ladies were all considered old enough and wise enough to decide, and also they had an academic degree so logical thinking should not present a problem. The other group was of the opinion that rational considerations only played a limited role in this. The job took over and occupied so much time that long-term plans were liable to be pushed aside. Was it not also the fault of the organization for allowing the workload to increase? Hence, the theme "balancing work-private life" should also be addressed at organizational level. The manager had, after all, been informed about the wish for children beforehand.

Most significant to the work satisfaction of the **production tiger** is attention and appreciation from management and colleagues. Especially recognition for their contributions by stars/hipos has a considerable effect on their work satisfaction.

A famous phrase from a Dutch cartoon figure is acutely applicable to production tigers: "It's no fun doing well in silence." There are no more nail-biting events that attract internal publicity, they are rarely discussed in important meetings, also because they provide little input for such meetings in the form of proposals or ideas, but nevertheless they form the backbone of the organization, the club that "keeps things ticking over," as they are often quick to point out. We should steer the production tigers away from becoming storytellers, for instance, by agreeing on when and how to make a T profile or on going into a Master-Trainee arrangement, or by deploying a different learning opportunity as mentioned in the previous chapter. All that with the aim of re-entering the production tiger into a trainee phase. Such arrangements naturally need to be put into the PCS.

Should the production tiger refuse to reorient his talents, should he still, despite everything, not want to cooperate with all these plans to avoid becoming a storyteller, then he should be kindly requested to leave the organization.

Finally, the **storytellers**. If we do things right there will hardly be any storytellers. Should they still be there, then it will be near impossible to get them to become productive again. But that does not mean they should be left to their own devices. Allowing them to slowly fade away can be expensive and shows poor management. They keep others from doing their work, mainly because they tend to be lengthy talkers. Managers who allow this to happen only make things worse, because storytellers know very well what is the matter with them and by letting it continue, they are more or less invited to continue their silly act. Mind you, the first-line managers, and hence the organization, have allowed this to happen by not taking the Human Talent Development decisions in the production tiger phase. Therefore, the organization is obliged to find a decent solution to the problem that they have created themselves. That can be done by providing for a socially respectable and financially rewarding parting handshake. Larger organizations may have options for storytellers to be retrained for a staff function, for instance as a lecturer in training. Although they must be careful to drop the unavoidable cynicism that comes with age. Another possibility is to turn them into auditors of both external and internal services or ... go into politics ... It can yield surprisingly good results.

Task # 5: Wanting to function as "heat shield"
The relative naivety of technical people – which means their relative inability to play political games – is often the reason for them putting great value on feeling good in an organization. Shared values, collective ambition, family feeling, sense of belonging, and sometimes also team spirit strongly influence concentration, creativity and productivity of technical professionals. Professionals want to be output-di-

Differentiate between managing and giving attention

STAR/HIPO	TRAINEE
– limit the number of innovation projects – avoid burn-out – monitor work/life balance – teach respect for the less talented	– give confidence but also: clear tasks and clear feedback – coach on the organizational culture – give short training periods in entirely different departments – stimulate assertiveness
PRODUCTION TIGER – render appreciation – give time and attention – avoid storytellership (with T profile, inverse Master-Trainee relation, training)	**STORYTELLER** – discover potential service-related qualities – retrain – or say goodbye

rected, and need peace and quiet to work on that. By peace and quiet we mean organizational peace and quiet, such as few changes in the management, few changes in the physical work environment (except for new gadgets), few structural and other organizational changes. None of those new, improved forms or screens where you have to click on something different every time. No more new lists and schedules with a slightly better layout, so you don't know where what is, no organizational rampage campaigns to improve the quality or to change the culture. What technical people don't mind at all is investments in further development of the collective ambition and the influx of new talent. Severely disturbing – and hence frustrating for both creativity and productivity – is the appointment of managers who do not have any background in what is actually taking place in the workplace.*

We mean managers who have no affinity with the discipline, who have not at the very least studied the discipline. Typically unrest reaches a climax on occasions when an economist, a lawyer, a psy-

---

* See also Chapter 4.

chologist, or even worse an MBAer becomes a first-line manager leading a group of doctors, engineers, historians, journalists, alpha-scientists, pedagogs, architects, cooks, or other artists. This source of unrest can, for some assertive professionals, even lead to anger: "The scientist/engineer sees the manager as a bureaucrat, paper shuffler and parasite, an uncreative and unoriginal hack who serves as an obstacle in the way of creative people trying to do a good job, and a person more interested in dollars and power than knowledge and innovation," Michael Badawy warned us back in 1982.* The higher the hierarchical level such a manager enters, the less of a problem he is, provided the organization has no center-of-excellence ambition but merely wants to perform as a middle-of-the-road company. You can indeed achieve the latter with professional managers because they see the organization first and foremost as a money-making machine that can and must be optimized. But most professional organizations find middle-of-the-road performance too meager an option. Those organizations would do better not to allow economists, organizational specialists, or MBA managers within a radius of two miles. As a manager of a service department such as HR or finance, yes, but nowhere else. At Philips Electronics R&D they knew this very well. When I (MW) worked there, the same discussion came up every once in a while during a board meeting. They would then try to imagine what it would be like if a non-physicist became CEO. Or they tried to imagine an electrical engineer, a mathematician, a mechanical engineer or a chemical engineer as CEO. Words like economist, lawyer, and MBA never came up during these discussions.

Professionals need peace and quiet, because the half-value time of knowledge is decreasing dramatically, making the discipline change continuously; and the more a discipline changes, the more there is a need for a constant factor, for something that does not change, something that can function as a refuge. The work environment – in other words, the organization – can be that refuge. Philips Electronics' research department has been in the same location for more than 80 years, with the board of directors for many years on the fifth floor and

---

* Michael Badawy is professor of Technology and Strategic Management at New York University, and former student of Edwards Deming and Peter Drucker.

the gatekeepers have been there long enough so that they can check most of the 1,500 employees in and out by name when they enter or leave the premises, initially by bicycle and later by car.

The origin of the phrase "heat shield" originates from the manager of the Philips research laboratory. When asked what he thought was the most important thing for him to do, he said: "Making sure that the hens keep laying eggs." He explained: "What I mean is that I want to function as a kind of heat shield, protecting my people from the corporate noise of the support functions, division managers, Board of Directors, etc. I deflect that noise via my heat shield right back to where it came from, because if I let it get through, the hens stop laying eggs."

He held his left hand horizontally in front of his chest and made a U with his right hand visualizing the direction of the noise coming down to the bottom of the U and then going straight up again.

Even as a senior executive, he would keep all possible distractions away from his workforce, even to the extent that, if necessary, he would fill out their time sheets.

It was later discovered that the more senior managers – 50 years plus – are more prepared to function as such a heat shield. The main reason for this is that at that age, managers are more concerned about their current job than about their next one. They know that the chance they will make the Board is remote or they have lost the ambition and hence they concentrate more than before on the ins and outs of the part of the organization that they lead. Younger managers "on their way to the top" are generally more concerned about their next job than the present one. Hence, they are more inclined to play the game and do what they are told from above or by corporate support functions. Very often it involves changing or raising the bureaucratic load through the introduction of all sorts of vertical planning & control rules, by imposing accountability and by making parameters more transparent (See Chapter 1 for a listing of such rules and procedures). Because planning & control is not sexy enough, younger managers are more inclined to delegate this quickly and thus make "the hens stop laying eggs altogether." (see the examples in Chapter 1: Much ado at Casey Labs, "... yes but nothing has been filled out!" and "long live the random generator.")

Regrettably there are only few organizations where assertive, slightly disobedient (but despite that collective ambition-loving) young managers stand a good chance of being selected for a vacant higher management position. The related advantages – like constructive friction, innovation, entrepreneurship, avoid groupthink*, etc. – are usually marginalized. No troublemakers please! Anglo-American short-term focused organizations prefer to surround themselves with conformists, sycophants, and yes-men. If you buy the same brand of car as the top dog and wear suspenders like him then you move up even faster.

Some knowledge-intensive organizations think that the unrest caused by management reduces if you tell the professionals how management works. In hospitals, they call that management participation. The effect turns out to be very limited and thus of little use; doctors prefer to be doctors and the patients of course like it that way. Moreover, such investments tend to make energy flow in the wrong direction. Professional expertise must not be diluted with management stuff, because it is a waste of what is now called "intellectual capital." Instead of that, we must enrich the light baggage of the non-expert manager with the principles of the discipline of the professionals that he is about to manage. In particular, the abstract jargon of the ever-infringing corporate economists is virtually meaningless to most professionals. In their day-to-day work they do not meet people who they see as cops and they do not think in terms of transaction costs, etc. A discipline-loving professional is not in this world to increase NPV, ROI and ROACE. He is there to explore, describe, explain, predict, design and help. He wants to extract secrets from Mother Nature, find answers to difficult questions, and make things that work. Creating increased shareholder value is the least of his concerns. In short, of all the concerns that are irrelevant to most professionals, the theories of economics possess the highest level of disturbing potential while in a pragmatic sense they have the least to offer.

---

* Groupthink is a form of self-censuring whereby critical information is kept back by certain group members because they think that it is not considered relevant to the others or because they are afraid of an unpleasant confrontation.

Task # 6: Practice a commanding but servant attitude

No matter how you look at it, a manager must have authority, otherwise he cannot lead. The trouble – for some – is that you cannot buy authority. You must earn it from the people who have been entrusted to you. You get it when you are high enough in the hierarchy to possess a lot of "carrot and stick" power, or when you know what the work in the workplace is really all about, in which case you have expert power. If the latter component is missing, managing professionals becomes difficult. Decisions made by someone who does not know the business i.e. accepting things on a hierarchical basis only, is difficult for the average professional. He does not perceive being higher up in the hierarchy as a valid argument for him to obey. "A professional organization is an organization where the base is the boss." (Hanke Lange).

To give someone more power by placing him in a higher position is easily done but to make someone more knowledgeable takes much more time and effort. So a person who has no clue about the business generally finds it difficult to manage. That applies most to the first-line manager, the first level of management above workers on the floor. Make sure he knows the business. Do not necessarily select him from among the best professionals – that would be a waste – but he must have studied the discipline and read the professional literature. For instance, it is impossible for an economist or lawyer to qualify the effort of a software engineer, or negotiate the viability and challenge of the annual targets that a surgeon or a physician has put down in his PCS. Chances are that these people will be led astray by the professionals. First of all because often a discipline has its own quality standards and ethics and does not tolerate interference based on someone's hierarchical position. And second – as said before – because professionals are not inclined to accept work-related decisions from a "layman." The boss, for them, is not just right because he's the boss.

So doctors must be led by doctors, teachers by teachers, judges by judges, chefs by chefs, engineers by engineers, and priests by priests. It is even better if the second tier and the levels above are filled by professional experts, like in the Catholic Church and the German car industry.

Engineers, asparagus and spaghetti

The two largest Dutch companies, Shell and Philips Electronics, have recently both appointed an engineer as CEO. The accountant and the retailer respectively, have been replaced by people who know about the business they run and that is very reassuring. The beauty about engineers is that they are not afraid of market analysts, shareholders, and spaghetti organizations, and that is because they have learned a real trade. That is why they realize that there is real value and synergy in professionals working together in the primary process and not by shuffling bonds or designing symmetrical structure diagrams.

Engineers are used to designing, making things function, and constantly improving and renewing properties of complex substances and systems that are generally needed to make life fun: bulbs, computers, concert halls, nylon, aspirin, contact lenses, etc. Many disciplines, departments, business units, and suppliers have to work together to make these complex things. If as a top executive you do not understand why that collaboration is needed, if you do not see the synergy, then you are liable to structure your organization into something that looks like a plate with asparagus. It looks very nice and you can deal with each stalk of asparagus separately. However, asparagus does not interact like spaghetti. A non-technical person does not see that disadvantage. Managers educated in economics look at the market (even if they don't know whether it really exists) and love planning & control and counting money. Probably a good line of attack for running a call centre or a restaurant, a bank or a cookie factory but not for running a technology-intensive organization.

It is often said that engineers lack social and communication skills and that they are relatively naive, but they know what it is about and that is what counts!

The Anglo-American business model knows two disciplines that the Rhineland tradition does not recognize as serious – and certainly not scientific – specializations. One is "making money with money" (the virtual trade in virtual paper with a virtual value) and the other one is "managing." With regard to the latter, people in the US have succeeded in developing a quasi-academic program that prepares people for management positions in the industry, without the students studying the technical disciplines on which the industry is based: physics, chemistry, electronics, mechanical engineering, IT, etc. In this so-called Master of Business Administration (MBA) program, students learn about profit maximization, to satisfy shareholders, and to measure knowledge. They are also trained in *planning & control*, in making rational analyses, and in changing "the organization" (= merge departments, sell off components, make alliances, execute efficiency drives, change the mindset and so on). They also learn another language. A language full of esoteric jargon that is meant mainly to strengthen the MBA culture and the group feeling amongst managers. A characteristic of that language is that it is totally divorced from the language that workers on the floor use. "Floor talk" is down to earth, robust, direct, and linked to the applied technology, the production processes, and the specific products being produced. MBA jargon is abstract and trendy, and can be used in any organization, regardless of what is being made. Feltmann says about this: "What has their full attention is a set of spoken and written texts (meetings, discussions, emails, telephone calls, dossiers, reports, letters, etc.). And those texts are about 'fabrications' like goals, structures, routes, projects, competencies, clusters, policy plans, coaching, annual reports, careers, peer review, board of directors, customers, market, merger partners, IT, 'it is important that ...,' 'why don't we quickly ...,' etcetera, etcetera, etcetera. It is never about acoustic impedance, blood pressure, chromatic aberration, plastic foil, electron microscope, formation permeability, Young's module, porosity, capillary pressure, geo-mechanical parameters, polymerization, acceleration, traction, drying, welding, grinding and temperature.

Looking at this from the Rhineland work culture, MBA graduates are dangerous. Mainly because they have been taught that good management decisions are based on quantitative analyses. That is a mistake, because not everything that counts in an organization is quantifiable. In the Rhineland tradition, a filing case with graphs and tables is not a real business. A real business is run by real people who can also react irrationally and intuitively, who sometimes need more attention and sometimes less, who can be creative one time and useless the next, who love their work one day and hate it the next. In an interview, Henry Mintzberg said that MBA schools usually give the impression that human skills and particularities hardly seem to matter. When MBA graduates make plans and prepare beamer presentations, read studies and reports, process and analyze all sorts of data, they think they are managing. According to Mintzberg, you can recognize effective managers by their subtle behavior, their forcefulness, and their involvement with the people in the organization. They know what workers on the floor find important because they know the business. They feel personally instead of formally responsible. That sounds rather Rhineland, in the sense that the guild master from the old days would have no problem agreeing with such a job description.

The Rhineland management style of Anton Philips

The manager of an industrial enterprise must:
1 Know how to select the right employees.
2 Convey his views to them and inspire them to work intensely together.
3 Be a financier, especially in abnormal times.
4 Possess legal insight.
5 Possess technical insight (to be able to fend off and stay ahead of the competition).
6 Possess a great sense of tact and justice.
7 Look after his employees, and provide for relaxation and education.
8 Timely seize land and assess building plans.
9 Be flexible in times of crisis.
10 See managing a business not as a task but as a sport.
Anton Philips at the award ceremony of his honorary doctorate from the Rotterdam Business School in 1928.

Without relevant knowledge you cannot get there

When asked for advice by an organization that is new to me, I always first want to spend a few days walking around and talking to the people in the workplace. Getting to know the Primary Process because that is what it is all about. Without it there is no organization. That is where most of the added value is. The new CEO did not understand why he was not taken seriously as the boss. Professionals would not listen to him and refused to interact, and then when he did make a decision it would often not be followed. The management had told staff that I was coming and what I wanted and had even drawn up a time schedule covering the two days (first here from 9 am to 11 am then there from 11 to 12, then lunch, etc.). They had even given staff my resume. During my round I asked a group of lab technicians what they were most proud of. One of them said: "Mr Weggeman, we want to show you a gear wheel which is unique, what it can do is really close to a miracle, do you want to see it work, after all you are an engineer." I considered it an honor and thought at the same time: "Indeed but will I be able to appreciate the miracle I am about to see and recognize what it does that is so special?" The men took me to a test stand, switched it on and placed me in front of it. I thought it was great but could not figure it out. The thing hummed. There were numerous recorders attached to it that showed steady climbing ranges of figures or slowly oscillating around a middle value. There was water cooling, it smelled a bit of oil, small weights went up and down and I thought it was wonderful, at least in an aesthetic way. As it turned out later, they had been watching my non-verbal reactions to find out if I "saw" it. And apparently I had shown the right reactions because afterwards they confided in me and one of them said: "We've got a new boss, an MBA. We showed him the test bench when he came and he did not see a damn thing! Then Bill here asked him to make it easier: 'Have you ever seen a seized bearing?' He hadn't! We make 30,000 of them a day! 'I didn't know that bearings could seize,' he added. Thought it was funny I guess. And that man is going to manage us? We have not seen him here again. Are you surprised that when yet another decision whirls down on us from the fancy offices upstairs we tell each other: 'Leave it be!'?"

There was a moment of silence after which I shook hands and thanked them for the kind reception. "Good luck with your task," said one of them. "It won't be easy."

The manager of a group of professionals will be draped with authority when he is from the same profession, or at the very least he has studied it. If that condition is fulfilled, then there is another danger lurking, the manager is tempted to use his hierarchical position to push through his opinion based on his professional expertise. Chances are that his arguments will not be convincing enough. Instead of investigating further how it is precisely, it is tempting for him to play the "the-boss-is-right" game rather than the "he-who-knows-is-right" game. Each time a first-line manager goes for that easy way out, his authority erodes further, with the ultimate consequence that the professionals stop taking him seriously and will also use their talents to fool you. They will, in a clever way, let you believe that they do what you want them to do, but will simply continue doing it their way. Not a nice situation.

It is particularly necessary to take the professional authority of the manager seriously during discussions about decisions initiating new projects, and the progression and required steering or termination of current activities. Managers must enjoy the results that are achieved by the people who have been entrusted to them. Based on his ability, he will gain motivation to continue to serve and facilitate. The first-line manager in particular does not always like to delegate those projects that are the most interesting and challenging tasks, because he wants to play a decisive role in the work on fascinating professional problems. It is mainly the young and freshly appointed managers coming straight from the ranks who are prone to this temptation. Such a manager experiences the facilitating contribution that people expect him to make as insignificant. He does not see anything creative in motivating and stimulating professionals working on a nice project; they are already intrinsically motivated. Hence, it becomes essential for his functioning as a first-line manager to enjoy the achievements of his people, without actually making a tangible contribution. In the same way, parents can take pleasure in the achievement of their children and a football coach in the victory of his team. As Herbert Simon says: "Creative managers are people who can receive great satisfaction from creative outcomes even when their role in producing those outcomes has been an indirect one – specifically: a managerial one."

And, like so many things in management land, subservient leadership is nothing new, in the words of Lao-Tse 600 years before Christ: "A leader is best when people barely know he exists, not so good when people obey and acclaim him, worst when they despise him. But of a good leader, who talks little, when the work is done, his aim fulfilled, they will say: we did it ourselves."

"*Dass sagt sich so leicht, dass lebt sich so schwer,*" (Easier said than done), German singer Hildegard Knef once sang, because the ego is often an obstacle.

Showing off someone else's achievement as your own and what it can lead to ...

A young, very talented industrial designer, who worked at a large multinational, had made a new revolutionary invention. When he showed it to his boss, he said: "Great. I'll put it on the agenda of the next International Product Design Meeting, but you'll also have to put my name on it. This design is so exceptional and innovative that it can go two ways in that meeting, either they will jump on the table out of enthusiasm, or run it into the ground entirely. In the latter case, I can take the rap, and if they are enthusiastic the credit will go to you." The young designer thought it a bit strange, however that was apparently how things were done. A few days later, before the documents had to be sent to the meeting, his boss told him: "I have done some probing about what they think of your design, and if I'm right in my assessment, I rate the chance of acceptance as no higher than 20%. But I think it is good that I have it kept on the agenda anyway, but without your name on it. You have a whole career ahead of you and if it turns sour, someone in my position can take it. After a lot of thought the young man agreed. After all he thought it is more important that his design was put on the agenda than that the right name was mentioned. The Design Meeting took place and everyone was standing on the table applauding loudly. This was the best design they had seen in years. The boss got all the credit. The following day he organized a little departmental celebration at the end of the day to mark the success. There was champagne and sushi and the young designer was heralded by the boss as the new hero. If only everyone could be so daring in their design, so creative and so involved in the organization. Except: outside the department no one knew the real story and so the notion was still that the design originated from the boss himself. Three months after the incident the young designer resigned. He went to work for a newly established design bureau that became very successful. Later, two more of his colleagues made the same move.

As Indira Gandhi said: "My Grandfather once told me that there were two kinds of people: those who do the work and those who take the credit. He told me to try to be in the first group; there was much less competition."

The Breuker-Van 't Hek formula for professional quality
(based on years of experience)

$$K = \frac{E \times P}{I}$$

E = effort; number of working hours (quantitative)
P = professionality; the quality of each hour
    (= expertise x social/communication skills)
I = influence of the ego; range: 1 to 10;
    1 = serving, totally non-egocentric,
    10 = maximum chest beating: me, me, me

It is bizarre to note that many managers in their "role" as parent do exercise the required modesty and subservient attitude. Say for instance your daughter comes home with a good report card and short-

---

* From Engbert Breuker, CEO of Pentascope, and Tom van 't Hek, hockey coach and sports commentator

ly after at a family gathering you tell her: "show your report card to granny and aunty. Show them how well you have done." Few fathers will push their daughter aside and address the family saying: "Ladies and gentlemen may I have your attention please. Thanks to the well-balanced upbringing by Sacha and me, our little daughter Angelica has again managed to do very well as you can tell by her report card." Parents don't do that. You know very well what you did to motivate your daughter to study, and how you helped her to do that, but you do not want to tell the world. You leave the honor to your daughter and humbly enjoy the results she has achieved. Funnily enough, many of those fathers, when they get to the office the next morning act so differently.

Lama Govinda said that at some point each individual has to make a choice between striving to understand power and striving for power.

In oriental cultures, spiritual hierarchy is determinative. The lower positioned are central because they still have a lot to learn, they go first because their road is longer.

In the occidental hierarchy, the highest positioned are central, unfortunately not because they have still a lot to learn but because they have most power. That structure hierarchy is based on a ranking of functional-dependent responsibilities and hence rewards role congruent behavior over wisdom. That is why it is better to continue realizing that working high up in the hierarchy is just working high up in the hierarchy, because the work needs to be done anyhow.

We can summarize this chapter as follows:

Managing knowledge-intensive organizations requires:
- Developing a collective ambition together
- Inspiring people
- Being there, observing well and really communicating
- Daring to differentiate (= output-based management unless ...; acting assertively to people who are not so good at their profession any more)
- Wanting to function as a heat shield against "noise from above"
- Exercising an authoritative but subservient attitude

"Man with head in clouds
not has feet on ground,
unless very tall man"

Tatanka-Iyotanka or "Sitting Bull" (1831-1890),
pragmatic, Sioux chief of the Lakota Indians.
Defeated in 1876 with 3,500 indians in self-managing teams,
the Seventh Cavalry of General Custer at Little Bighorn River.

7 ORGANIZATIONAL CULTURE

Stimulate a climate in which professionals are trusted and given room to exploit and explore their profession

Cultural characteristics of knowledge-intensive organization

The attention for organizational culture increased considerably when Peters and Waterman discovered in 1982 that successful organizations stand out partly for their focused, strong and deep penetrating culture. An important cultural characteristic that they found in most of these excellent organizations was "freedom in solidarity": an optimum combination of consistent, inspired, mission-driven leadership and individual autonomy. On the one hand, those organizations had a small number of explicit values and standards that were strongly enforced; on the other, they expected employees to think innovatively, take initiative, and act in an entrepreneurial manner.

On the basis of the literature and experiences gained by working, managing and advising knowledge-intensive organizations, we have identified the following seven cultural characteristics of knowledge-intensive organizations.

What is a knowledge-intensive organization and what are knowledge workers?

A knowledge-intensive organization is an organization with knowledge workers in the primary process (or at the very least in the technical staff provided it has a dominating influence on the functioning of the primary process).

At a knowledge-intensive organization, professionals are busy making an inventory of knowledge, to develop, to divide, to apply and to evaluate it in order to realize the organization's goals and to satisfy internal and external clients and themselves.

Knowledge workers are usually college graduates. They are employees for whom the production factor knowledge (brains) is more important than the production factor physical labor (muscles). Knowledge workers must – compared to production workers – learn continuously if they are to do their work adequately.

1 Lack of collective focus

When you ask professionals on the floor what the organizational mission, vision, goals or strategies are, their answers will have two things in common: 1) they don't know the difference between the four terms, and 2) everyone says something else.

Knowledge workers are in many cases more involved in their work than in the organization. For them, mission, vision, goals and strategies fall under the category of management speak and therefore it is a waste of time to pay much attention to the distinction between these four strategic terms. Whatever the professional is doing at that time *is* the strategy, and when he is finished with that the organization has reached its goal. Similar to: "L'organisation? C'est moi!" Professionals that practice this attitude are known as cosmo pros, those who do this to a lesser extent: local pros.*

The cosmo pro versus the local pro

Cosmo pro		Local pro
low	loyalty to the organization	high
high	commitment to their own specialization	functional
high	orientation on external reference groups	low
no	interested in a management position	some

A dominant external orientation, for instance on the discipline group, is called a cosmo-political orientation. We refer to greater focus on the internal organization as local orientation. These two orientations are one dimensional, mutually excluding extremes. The extremes are rare, but most knowledge workers do have a preference: 60-40, 70-30, 80-20. A cosmo-politically inclined professional has lower loyalty to the organization, higher loyalty to his own specialization, a stronger focus on external reference and little interest in a

---

* Realin, 1985

management position. On the other hand, a local pro generally has relatively high loyalty, a functional involvement in his own specialization, a weaker focus on external reference groups, and generally some interest in a management position.

The cosmo pro has no problem in moving to an organization where he has more freedom and possibilities to show his expertise and to develop. Offer him a bigger machine and two more assistants and he is gone. The cosmo pro generally finds colleagues within his discipline more interesting than colleagues elsewhere within the organization. For the cosmo pro, the level of his salary is a measure of the way his work is appreciated in the market. They are strong-headed knowledge workers who are mainly loyal to their discipline and their own talents, and much less to their employer.

The local pro is more involved in the organization than in his discipline. When the discipline is no longer important to the organization, the local pro is more inclined to wonder how he can contribute to the realization of the company's goals, rather than go looking for alternatives elsewhere. The readiness to re-educate is relatively large ("I have found a new challenge"). Given his involvement in the organization, the local pro finds it appealing at a certain moment to take on a management position. They like to reason that: "If the organization asks me, then I will do that, and I will largely leave my discipline behind."

The 10 commandments for the cosmo pro

1. Stay emotionally aloof
2. Do not get attached to an organization; practice detachment
3. Remain visible to the market
4. Arrange the home situation in such a way that it does not impede your mobility
5. Invest in your resume and consider a phone call from an agent as the beginning of a new adventure
6. Participate in many networks
7. Explore your potential capabilities and learn to learn
8. Avoid over-specialization
9. Avoid assignments with a time frame of more than two years
10. Ensure that, despite all that, you remain credible in the organization where you now work.

If you want to be a cosmo pro, you must be good at your job. The ideal is, of course, an organization with local pros who are so good that they can warrant a cosmo pro attitude, but do not do that because they feel at home in the club they work for, have a sense of belonging, family feeling, shared values.

Test: which of the aforementioned four parameters offers the greatest chance to reach that ideal situation? Right: "loyalty to the organization," thus investing in the development of a collective ambition! We have come full circle!

2 The reference frame for (management) decisions is outside one's own organization

Debating with professionals about what is and what is not true in the discipline takes time and is almost impossible if you do not belong to the discipline. If the one who starts the discussion has no more to offer than "management," then such a discussion is a waste of time ...

The layman does not know what he does not know

"The specialist has a bad character. Start a casual discussion, talk about something that he is not familiar with and he will answer you. You can continue, convinced that he is a decent human being. But when coincidence or a desire to please takes you to what he calls his specialization he remains silent. He smiles and lets you talk. Quiet and unashamed he waits until you are finished. He will not interrupt, because from your accumulation of mistakes, a deeper truth will emerge for him: he knows."
(Henri Bergson: *L'Evolution créatrice*. Paris, 1907)

The truth about what is technically right or wrong cannot be found internally. Rather, the trade organization, the scientific collegiums and the informal peer-group networks are the ones that indicate what is allowed or not, what the recommended methods, techniques and protocols are and what is old, not valid, unreliable or not done. "I do understand that management decision and of course it may be faster that way and as a result it may be cheaper, but I cannot cooperate with the implementation of that decision because my trade organization is opposed to it. We do not consider the approach responsible to the customer for the following reasons: (...) There is also the chance that if we follow that approach there will be complications:

(...) The statistics are very clear on this. In short: I will not risk my specialist credentials and therefore refuse to work that way."

Thus the decision-making culture at a knowledge-intensive organization is rather diffuse. Furthermore, the meaning of decisions taken is problematic, certainly where it concerns decisions that regard the execution of the profession, which for professionals is all too often the case. They are very resourceful at arguing that certain decisions, which at face value are unrelated to their profession, are nevertheless of decisive influence on the way they exercise their profession. Decisions about, for example, a room division, new opening hours for the company restaurant or the introduction of name badges therefore effortlessly translate into major impediments to the execution of the profession or in efforts to try to undermine the directives of the trade organization.

The profession is what it's all about. The rest is nonsense and you're even allowed to enjoy it

In the 1980s, the Board of Philips decided that everyone had to wear a badge with his name, the number of the building they were allowed to enter and a color code that indicated the level of the security risk the person in question posed: blue for staff, green for guests, and red for externals. The whole thing was completed with a photograph. Badges also had to be worn forthwith in the R&D laboratory. That, however, did not come about without a struggle. First of all, there was the Coordination Committee (CoCo) who wanted to know more about the motives. The CoCo was a kind of student-like body that periodically liaised with management mostly about unimportant things like the space between coat hangers in the cloak room, taking into account the average rainy days and the fact that most people came to work by bike. The CoCo asked for a special meeting with management: the first question was why badges had to be worn all of a sudden. The plant manager said something about security; a number of letters had been received with threats of attacks and that the measure was for all Philips employees in the Netherlands and that included the R&D laboratory. Of course, the CoCo was not at all convinced and pointed out the dangers that are inherent in wearing a badge. Most researchers did not were suits, so they could not attach the badge to the breast pocket or lapels. That meant that the badge had to worn on a ribbon around the neck and that way it could easily get caught in a gear box or in a tank with aggressive chemicals. Considerable hazards were looming and these hazards were deemed to be even more hazardous by the CoCo than the terrible things they had brought up before to get management to ban neckties. When the plant manager said it was not all that bad they went to the chairman of the board asking him: "Do you think that if we wear badges we will do better research?" The chairman did not think so but admitted that he was not sure, whereupon the CoCo said: "then we won't wear it, because for the last 80 years we have worked very successfully here without badges and we cannot rule out that if we wear the badge now our research will suffer." The discussion went on and a mutually agreeable decision could not be reached. The plant manager did not give up and threatened with sanctions: if you did not wear the badge you would not be able to pay in the company restaurant. The researchers interpreted this to mean that from now on you could get a free lunch if you removed your badge at the right moment.

Then, at a given moment, something happened which, in situations like this, must take place if the professionals are to support a decision from the top for which they can find no logic: an appeal to the relationship that the people have with each other based on their involvement with the organization. In the last two minutes of a "Thursday morning presentation session" (a popular weekly gathering where three researchers would present their work for 20 minutes each) the chairman took to the stand and said: "Friends, the Board will visit us on Monday. Please do me a favor and wear those badges, otherwise I'll be in trouble." And from that moment on the badge was worn. The deadlock was broken and the explanation given to the chairman was: "He did not say why we must wear it. But he is one of us and a good guy and we don't want him to get into trouble." Many researchers first wore the badge on their backs because: "Everybody knows what I look like from the front."

Characteristics of decision-making processes about non-technical issues

- Decision-making takes long due to
  - delay in the process is – justified or not – legitimized prioritizing "the work for the customer": "The phone's ringing. That is the customer. I must go."
  - discussions are started each time from scratch
- Tomorrow there is always more, other and better information than today
  - a discussion, a book, a seminar, …
  - "I have thought about it and maybe it's better if …"
- A diverging opinion and assessment phase can, all of a sudden, be followed by an unexpected convergence phase
  - "I have said what had to be said, I have pointed out the consequences and I have given alternatives. Now it is up to you," or: "Other than that, I am loyal."

- Implementing decisions already taken by management is not interesting and has the lowest priority for the professional
  - "We will do that when we have time, during Christmas or the Summer break."

3 Professionals base work distribution on personal preferences

Professionals are inclined to divide the world into "good guys & bad guys." When a new and unexpected task arrives, they prefer to give it to a good guy/hipo who is already snowed under with work. New colleagues can be surprised about that: "Why not Archibald? He doesn't have much on his hands right now." "Yes, and you know why that is? Think about it! If we give it to him then he turns it into a project with all bells and whistles, asks a million questions, bothers you with all sorts of half products and interim results, has to go to LA three times to discuss things there and in the end we get nothing. No, we will ask Bill; and yes he is busy but giving him one more task will not make any difference to him." And that is why the good guys get busier and busier while the bad guys do less and less.

Knowledge workers must constantly want to learn!

The car is one of the most over-engineered products of modern time. Innovations to engine, transmission, chassis, and bodywork are nowadays always improvements and seldom renewals. We go from 1 to 2 to 3 airbags and from 8 via 16 to 24 valves. Also, the surroundings in which the car does its work have not changed much. There is more technology at crossings and there is more traffic. That's about it.

That is why a proposal from the central drivers' licenses authority in the Netherlands suggesting that drivers should do regular training does not make much sense. "The driver's license for life is going to disappear," they predict. "Interim re-training is necessary to keep our knowledge and skills up to date." However, if nothing fundamental changes in the car nor in traffic, what is that training going to be about? Learning psychology tells us that in a stable situation the following rule applies: the more you practice, the better you get. There are few people who play the piano an hour a day, who gradually play worse and worse. Most skills develop by frequent repetition. And people who buy a car but never drive it need to follow a totally different course.

We can use our energy more efficiently debating the necessity for re-education of dentists, surgeons, IT specialists, engineers, architects and the like. They have to work with methods, techniques, and equipment

that become obsolete almost as soon as you have just managed to understand them. It has become more and more an illusion to think that these
knowledge workers can handle everything in their careers based on the
knowledge acquired at university. If you have never learned when setting
a stent is appropriate and how to do that, you will simply keep doing by-
pass surgery.

In short, there are two alternatives for knowledge workers. You arrange your work so that there is sufficient time to learn, in order to stay
ahead. Or you go into management. Like driving a car, managing is a skill
that has hardly changed over the last 50 years. So if you are a technician
who suffers from learning stress, make sure that you become the boss of
something. Then you only have to bother with planning and control of
time and money, which hasn't changed since the invention of capitalism.

Knowledge workers know full well who among them is good at what.
So they also know who is not so good (anymore) at something and
who is not good at anything. A professional knows somewhat less
about himself; he generally rates himself just that bit higher than colleagues would rate him.

A few times during large-scale training programs for professionals, I experimented with setting up such a ranking. It turned out that
the question of *what* you rank must be formulated very precisely and
in great detail. The first time I asked: who in Europe is the best specialist in removing an appendix from patients older than 55? That is a
far too general a question for professionals to answer. I had to ask:
who in Europe is the best specialist in removing the appendix from
patients older than 55, who also have problems with ischemia colitis
and diabetes and you do not have a Gamma Knife at your disposal?
Now they can do something with a question like that. The answers
came immediately: "Then you have to go to Van den Berg in Groningen and if he is too busy go to Van de Kersemaeckere in Louvain, as
the second best." The experience is that the standard deviation in
those types of rankings is close to zero. The same people are always at
the bottom. And when I then ask how we should deal with the low
ranked, there is a deathly silence. There is some shuffling of chairs
until someone says: "HR! HR must do something. Nothing to do
with us." Colleagues nod their heads, everyone is relieved. The "danger" is gone: it is not their cup of tea.

But it really should be their business. Together they tell wonderful stories about peer reviews, boast about the professional disciplinary board, and have developed clever procedures for external visitations and accreditation of colleagues. But when push comes to shove, these things do not work. Because in most knowledge-intensive organizations flower power reigns among professionals. As long as my place on the ranking is OK. Knowledge-intensive organizations are often also rich enough to organize things around these lesser colleagues. "We can also see that he can't keep up with the fast development anymore, but he used to be great and helped us a lot. We have all learned from him. So let him fade out a bit." People talk in euphemistic terms about fading expertise of (older) colleagues. When I (MW) recently visited a law firm during an assignment, I asked one of the partners about one of his colleagues and asked: "Is he not that good anymore?" He answered: "He knows it, but lately the side effects of his functioning have become more apparent." And a manager of a trial area in a large engineering agency, answered to a similar question: "It is not that he does things wrong, but over the last few years a negative approach has gradually crept into his functioning."

In Chapter 6, we showed that an assertive approach of knowledge workers who are not so good at their profession anymore, is one of the most important tasks of the first-line manager. If he doesn't do it, nobody will, and everyone will become a storyteller in no time (see Chapter 5).

Soft healers ...

At an independent partnership of medical specialists, there were problems with the allocation of tasks and I (MW) was asked to make recommendations for solving the situation. In my tour around the specialists I also interviewed an artistically dressed gentleman of 56 years old. He attended the meetings of the associated hospitals on behalf of the partnership and his colleagues had instructed him to adopt a default position of "against," no matter what was on the agenda, because the partnership thought that the way things are going now is perfectly fine so everything the managers and administrators wanted to change, could only lead to things getting worse. He was also responsible for selecting art. The partnership had built a new ER a few years ago with a large auditorium-like waiting room where they could also hold art exhibitions. He decided on the annual exhibition program and organized it by inviting artists to exhibit their work. "I do not have much time for patients anymore," he said with a smile. When I told the chairman of the partnership that he had a very expensive person on the payroll taking minutes at meetings and looking after the auditorium he said: "You are right, but we cannot have him look after patients that much anymore because he is no longer very good at that. He finds it difficult to deal with modern methods and techniques. That is why we have chosen this solution. In three years he will retire and then we will take on a new young colleague and reallocate the work. Maybe he can retire earlier, we are thinking about it. He is taking some work off our hands isn't he?" "Don't you think he doesn't know what's going on?" I asked. After that, the tone of the discussion changed and together we looked into possibilities for the specialist to re-enter the mainstream activity, making a T profile or moving him into an inverted Master-Trainee relationship.*

Such a process cannot be started without telling the semi-retired what he should have been told long ago: that he is no longer that good at his job. Because that is not a nice thing to do and because they are not trained to conduct these kinds of discussions, they had organized things around him. The first honest discussion with the older specialist did not go well, as was expected, and both the chairman and I found ourselves out of his office in no time. The next discussion a week later went better. He had thought about the situation, had had a discussion at home and with friends, and he noticed that he gradually seemed to acknowledge that there was some truth in what we had told him before. The third meeting was constructive. "OK we will do this, but ...," and then there were the usual conditions. "We would recommend accepting these conditions if at all reasonable, because most of them are of secondary importance," "I want to keep my room," or "... I don't want Archibald to teach me these new methods," or "... but I want my 'white coat' monthly allowance again." In this case all conditions were accepted. The result was that all problems around the work allocation have disappeared and the old specialist has rediscovered the love for his work as a serious member of the team again.

---

4 In multidisciplinary collaboration, one's own discipline is often just that little bit more important

"Old news," you would say. "If there is one thing that's typical of professionals, it is the tedious and often even hostile way certain disciplines treat each other." The "weapons" deployed are closing ranks, jargon as an entry barrier, school ties, and the like. What possibly has some news value is the fact based on experience that that collabora-

---

* See for T profile and the inverted Master-Trainee relationship Chapter 5.

tion becomes more difficult if the disciplines are technically closer. That is difficult to explain to your grandmother, who will ask: "But if the disciplines are so alike than they should understand each other better." That is most probably the case, but that positive effect is heavily overshadowed by a strong phenomenon: territorial instinct and competition! If you are neighbors and you know how they play the game, you are more inclined to do the same thing. So the neighbors are building a fence to make sure you don't know exactly what is going on and they will make absolutely sure that their game is only played in their garden. We can see that with doctors and lawyers, orchestral musicians and journalists. All are claiming the exclusive rights to their specific contribution, and defining and guarding those rights is particularly relevant with respect to adjacent disciplines. So cardiologists and internists have more trouble with each other than any of those groups with surgeons, and the cellists and the violists more mutual hassle than with anyone in the brass section.

"It is easier for you to teach a sciences student to understand the beauty of Schiller and Goethe than a humanities student to understand the beauty of Maxwell's Laws."

On the other hand, there is often admiration for the skills of other adjacent professions, because from the next door garden in particular you can see how complicated, successful or beautiful the work is that the neighbors do. To save face, an effective strategy in those cases is to criticize the underlying theory. "It works but it's based on a very flimsy concept!"

5 A lot is done informally
Professionals are – despite bossy managers, eagle-eyed support services, and lots of guidelines and procedures – very skilled at taking care of their own business in their own way. The greater the level of bureaucracy, the higher the level of skill in the company and the lower the level workers' understanding for the manager, the more they are able to succeed. Professionals are well educated, generally have higher than average intelligence and thus know how they can responsibly "fool" the formal systems. Of course, with the alibi that the customer or client benefits and that is what it is all about. This is extensively explained in Chapter 1. The need to arrange informally what is

good for the customer appears to be one of the reasons why the mobility of medical specialists is so low, in comparison for instance with lawyers and accountants. Compared to the offices where the latter two work, hospitals are intricate organizations with specialized spaces with complicated high-tech machinery. It takes time to get to know the informal network and how to play the game. "Actually, the unit is full but I can arrange for another bed." "I've got someone here who ..." "If you can fit this patient in I'll take your shift next week." That attitude results in a more or less anarchistic but task-oriented collaboration culture in which result is much more important than following set procedures and filling out forms.

The problem is that the work culture which is often dominant in the primary process tends to spill over into support services and departments with no professionals but with people who mainly perform short-cyclical routine work. Every large knowledge-intensive organization has its "factory": the technicians at a microbiological laboratory, the financial department at an consultancy, the IT help desk at a university, the compressor maintenance department of a hospital, the draughtsman at an architectural firm, etc. These "factories" have a more production-oriented culture, which is, however, often threatened by the precipitated attraction of the organization's informal culture of the professional. Little can be done about that other than relocating the "factory" to a separate building to reduce the risk of "infection" by the professional culture. It would help to communicate explicitly to the people that routine "factory work" is different from the knowledge-intensive work of the professionals and that, therefore, a different regime applies. So create space for the professionals to let them work according to their own devices and make clear to others how vitally important that is to the organization as a whole. Each his own culture! That increases the chance of playing down the following stereotype images of the professional activity as perceived by the "factory" workers:
- It is one big playground there
- That's where the newly-exempted work
- I don't think anybody has a boss there
- They are always travelling
- They come and go as they please
- What will become of the company if they get to run things

- I can also write reports, but actually doing what they put in them, forget it!
- I can't really imagine that we need all these people to do that
- If something goes wrong, they'll just cheerfully start all over again

6 *On the floor there is low financial-economical awareness*
Professionals don't think you should spend too much time talking about strategy. There is only one good strategy ever since time began: there is always enough money for a good project! In professional science-oriented organizations they are even more convinced of that than in humanities-oriented knowledge-intensive organizations. So professionals see nothing wrong in going over budget and funding. For them, these are merely abstract figures that represent some sort of internal Mickey Mouse money. "If you turn that 9 into an 8 then we are within budget again and in reality nothing changes, so who can object?" Budget overruns are good because they show that the customers are better looked after or that more customers have been helped or that intended project results have been achieved, and *that* is what it is all about. After all, the aim of the organization is not to get the financial administration right, but to deliver good work, make new discoveries, solve problems, make things that work and fulfill promises made to the client. All the rest is secondary.

That is why professionals have high esteem for managers who always succeed in getting new money from somewhere. If they can do that, they are worshipped.

- Professional: "Boss, we can't do it. The only solution is to buy time on the Cray to do extended vector calculations."
- Boss: "Yes, but there is no more money. There is nothing left in the budget."
- Professional: "But don't you have a kitty somewhere?"
- Boss: "I'll see what I can do."

Bosses who can say that are good managers.

7 Left-brained professionals in particular create an atmosphere of openness and naivety

Certainly when it is about their profession, technical people are generally honest, consistent and to the point (= not social). Others who do not often use those qualities would call that naive. At a conference or exhibition, science-oriented (left-brained) professionals tell colleagues of a competing company enthusiastically how they have resolved a technical problem that the competitor is still working on. Not very clever for the company ("Can't do that! That way you're leaking expensive knowledge to the competition. Do they know how much getting a patent costs?"), but not bad for the world. Also, the colleagues of the other company would do the same thing so that in the end it's an equal contest. Managers think that is a rubbish argument and immediately start talking about IPR, CAs, NDAs, memos of understanding and other sorts of legal stuff. The truth, as always, is probably somewhere in the middle: Organization & Management is after all not a scientific profession and both professionals and their managers are right in their own way. The implication is that both should try to steer clear of extremes and adopt a middle course all the time. With the advance popularity of "open innovation" that task is not getting any easier for the managers.

The notion of professionals that everything that is true has to be told and the inclination of managers (the higher, the stronger that inclination) to classify that attitude as naive, can easily result in two sub-cultures that, at worst, can get disconnected because the fundamental way of looking at things does not fit any more. Respect for each other's way of seeing things can avoid getting into such a situation.

How a manger can use the naivety of the professional

I (MW) once asked the leader of a group of biologists how he could make those unyielding professionals do things his way. "By threatening with sanctions," he answered. "I say for instance: and if you have not pinned those butterflies by next week, I will deduct an amount from your pay." "Can you do that?" I asked. "I don't know but it works!" He even knew why it worked. It was in the words "an amount." "Some think it's five or ten dollars, others think it could be as much as 100 or 200 dollars."

This, then, is a sketch of mood characteristics that exist in and around knowledge-intensive organizations: below there are success factors for arriving at a productive collaboration culture:

- Respect for other disciplines (avoid field-specific jargon).
- Put the interests of the client first; after all, practical problems are blissfully unaware of the discipline classification we just happened to have made.
- Do not get distracted by pigeon-holing; dare to redirect, wanting to know who is good at what.
- Wanting to keep learning.
- Discard "knowledge = power and that = mine" attitude (sharing knowledge = multiplying knowledge = strength).
- Take the collective ambition seriously: either you are committed or "collective" does not concern you and you leave.

GRAND FINALE

*The essence of this book is typified by the following story**

It is a story about cross-border collaboration, professionals, state-of-the-art skills, knowledge sharing, creative tension, and new combinations, about collective ambition, modesty, involvement, self-organization and innovation, about output-based management, synergy, cultural integration, and a lot more. It is about musicians.

Past the pedestrian crossing, turn left, through the gate. As he slips the car keys into his pocket, he climbs the stairs and opens the door. "Good evening. Your name?" "Mason. David Mason." It is five to seven, Thursday evening, January 17th, 1967. EMI Studios. Abbey Road. London.

George Martin, producer of the Beatles, walks down the stairs in Studio Two. "David!" He shakes the hand of the smart-looking gentleman. Paul McCartney sees David. The same man, the same trumpet. On January 11th, McCartney watched an episode of BBC2's Masterworks series, a performance of Bach's 2nd Brandenburg Concerto. The following day Paul couldn't stop talking about it. "What was that little trumpet, it sounds great!" "A piccolo trumpet," said George Martin dryly, "and the man who plays it is David Mason, a friend of mine. I'll give him a call."

There is nothing. No score, no notes, no nothing. While he unpacks his trumpets, he hears: "Tada, tada, tatatata!" Paul McCartney sings how he wants it. George Martin takes notes. Sound technician Geoff Emerick places the microphones. The trumpet sounds through the big studio. John Lennon turns around.

* *VPRO TV guide*, week 6, 2007.

"Are you filming?" "No mate, that's how we always dress," says Lennon. David Mason looks at his yellow tie and purple trousers. It is five to twelve. He takes a final sip of tea and walks to the middle of the studio. Headphones on, trumpet at his lips. Second technician Phil McDonalds starts the tape.

The voice of Paul McCartney sounds through his head. *"In Penny Lane there is a barber showing photographs."* He waits. *"... it's a clean machine."* He quickly wets his lips. A short forceful breath and he begins. Exactly 16 seconds and 58 notes later, the trumpet shoots up to the *"blue suburban skies,"* the last and highest note. *"Penny Lane is in my ears and in my eyes ..."* Click. The tape stops. David Mason walks upstairs, trumpet in hand. "Better is impossible," he thinks. "Nice one, David, try one more time?" Deadly silence. George Martin throws an annoyed glance at McCartney. "Good God, you can't possibly ask the man to do that again. It was fantastic!" Long seconds. "OK David, thanks."

Quarter to twelve. The stately houses opposite are dark. David Mason crosses the pedestrian crossing into the London night. Tomorrow rehearsals again with his orchestra, the New Philharmonic.

Bibliography

Alkahafaji, A. and D. Tompkins (1990): Determinants and impact of organizational commitment. *Management Challenges.*

Allen, T. (1986): *Managing the Flow of Technology.* Boston: MIT Press.

Argyris, C. (1977): Double-loop learning in organizations. *Harvard Business Review,* September-October.

Badawy, M. (1982): *Developing Managerial Skills in Engineers and Scientists.* New York: Van Nostrand Reinhold.

Badawy, M. (1998): Managing human resources. *Research Technology Management,* September-October.

Bergson, H. (1907) *L'evolution créatrice.* Paris

Castells, M. (1985): *High Technology, Space and Society.* Beverly Hills: Sage.

Castells, M. (1998): *The Information Age: Economy, Society and Culture.* Cambridge: Oxford University Press.

Csikszentmihalyi, M. (2001): *Creativiteit, over flow, schepping en ontdekking.* Amsterdam: Boom. (in Dutch)

D'Aveni, R. (1994): *Hypercompetition: Managing the Dynamics of Strategic Manoeuvring.* New York: Free Press.

Davenport, T., et al. (1996): Improving knowledge work processes. *Sloan Management Review,* Summer.

Deal, T. and A. Kennedy (1982): *Corporate Cultures.* New York: Addison Wesley.

Den Hertog, F. en E. Huizinga (1997): *De kennisfactor; concurreren als kennisonderneming.* Deventer: Kluwer (in Dutch).

De Wit, H. (1998): *De lotus en de roos; Boeddhisme in dialoog met psychologie, godsdienst en ethiek.* Kampen: Kok Agora (in Dutch).

Drucker, P. (1993): *Post-capitalist Society.* Oxford: Butterworth-Heinemann.

Gibson, R. (1997): *Rethinking the Future*. London: Nicholas Brealey.

Goold, M. and A. Campbell (1987): *Strategies and Styles*. London: Basil Blackwell.

Hamel, G. and C.K. Prahalad (1994): *Competing for the Future*. Boston: Harvard Business School Press.

Hedlund, G. (1994): A model of knowledge management and the N-form corporation. *Strategic Management Journal*, 15.

Keuning, D., W. Opheij and H. Maas (1993): *Verplatting van organisaties*. Assen: Van Gorcum (in Dutch).

Luhmann, N. (1984): *Soziale Systemen, Grundriss einer allgemeinen Theorie*. Frankfurt am Main: Suhrkamp. (in German)

Maister, D. (1985): The one-firm-firm; what makes it successful. *Sloan Management Review*, Fall.

Maslow, A. (1954): *Motivation and Personality*. New York: Harper and Row.

Mintzberg, H. (1983): *Structures in Fives*. New Jersey: Prentice Hall.

Mintzberg, H. (1998): Covert leadership: notes on managing professionals. *Harvard Business Review*, november-december.

Mintzberg, H. and J. Quinn (1991): *The Strategy Process*. Englewood Cliffs: Prentice Hall.

Moss Kanter, R. (1985): Managing the human side of change. *Management Review*, April.

Nonaka, I. and H. Takeuchi (1995): *The Knowledge-creating Company*. New York: Oxford University Press.

Noordegraaf, M (1999): Wat zit er in het koffertje? Het verschil tussen onzekerheid en ambiguïteit. *M&O: Tijdschrift voor Organisatiekunde en Sociaal Beleid*, 53 (3) (in Dutch).

Peters, T. and R. Waterman (1982): *In Search of Excellence*. New York: Harper & Row.

Porter, M. (1985): *The Competitive Advantage*. New York: Free Press.

Porter, M. (1990): *The Competitive Advantage of Nations*. London: The Macmillan Press.

Prahalad, C.K. and G. Hamel (1990): The core-competence of the corporation. *Harvard Business Review*, May-June.

Realin, J. (1985): *The Clash of Cultures; Managers and Professionals*. Boston: Harvard Business School Press.

Root-Bernstein, R. (1989): Who discovers and invents. *Research Technology Management*, January-February.

Schmid, W. (2001): *Filosofie van de levenskunst*. Amsterdam: Ambo (in Dutch).

Schmidt, W. and B. Posner (1983): *Managerial Values in Perspective*. New York: American Management Association.

Schumpeter, J. (1942): *Capitalism, Socialism and Democracy*.

Shapero, A. (1985): *Managing Professional People: Understanding Creative Performance*. New York: Free Press.

Simon, H. (1986): How managers express their creativity. *Across the Board*, March.

Simon, H. (1993): Strategy and organizational evolution. *Strategic Management Journal*, 14.

Stacey, R. (1996): *Complexity and Creativity in Organizations*. San Fransisco: Berrett-Koehler.

Steiner, G. (2004): *Het oog van de meester*. Amsterdam: de Bezige Bij. (in Dutch)

Stengers, I. (1986): From the essay in the 1986 BSO Annual Report (in Dutch).

Treacy, M. and F. Wiersema (1995): *The Discipline of Market Leaders*. London: Addison-Wesley.

Van Amelsfoort, P. en G. Scholtes (1997): *Zelfsturende teams; ontwerpen, invoeren en begeleiden*. Oss: ST-Groep (in Dutch).

Verhoeven, A. (1999): *Information-seeking by general practitioners*. Groningen: Rijksuniversiteit Groningen.

Vermeulen Windsant, M. (1993): *De organisatie*. Amsterdam: de Bezige Bij (in Dutch).

Vermeylen, R. (2000): *Salto humano. Over samenwerken, leidinggeven en veranderen*. Schiedam: Scriptum (in Dutch).

Vernooy, R. (2000): *Honderd gezichten op een houding*. Amsterdam: Contact (in Dutch).

Weggeman, M. (1992): *Leidinggeven aan professionals*. Deventer: Kluwer (in Dutch).

Weggeman, M. (2000): *Kennismanagement: de praktijk*. Schiedam: Scriptum (in Dutch).

Weggeman, M. (2001): *Kennismanagement: Inrichting en besturing van kennisintensieve organisaties*. Schiedam: Scriptum (in Dutch).

Weggeman, M. (2003): *Provocatief adviseren; organisaties mooier maken*. Schiedam: Scriptum (in Dutch).